T0161513

THE PEAR AS ONE EXAMPLE

THE PEAR
AS ONE EXAMPLE

New & Selected Poems
1984—2008

Eric Pankey

AUSABLE PRESS
2008

Cover art: "Dreamer," by Jill Moser
2006. Oil on canvas. 40 x 40 inches. Private collection.
Photo by Ellen Page Watson.
Reproduced with the kind permission of the artist.

Design and composition by Ausable Press
The type is Granjon.
Cover design by Rebecca Soderholm

Published by
Ausable Press
1026 Hurricane Road
Keene, NY 12942
www.ausablepress.org

Distributed to the trade by
Consortium Book Sales & Distribution
1045 Westgate Drive
Saint Paul, MN 55114-1065
(651) 221-9035
(651) 221-0124 (fax)
(800) 283-3572 (orders)

The acknowledgments appear on page 273 and constititute a
continuation of the copyright page.

Library of Congress Cataloging-in-Publication Data

Pankey, Eric
The pear as one example : new and selected poems, 1984—2008 / Eric Pankey
p. cm.
ISBN 978-1-931337-39-7 (pbk. : alk. paper)
I. Title.

PS3566.A575P43 2008
811'.54—dc22
2007049674

For Jennifer and Clare

Also by Eric Pankey

Reliquaries 2005

Oracle Figures 2003

Cenotaph 2000

The Late Romances 1997

Apocrypha 1991

Heartwood 1988

For the New Year 1984

from APOCRYPHA (1991)

from THE LATE ROMANCES (1997)

from CENOTAPH (2000)

from ORACLE FIGURES (2003)

For the New Year (1984)

TO OLGA KNIPPER

May 25, 1901 (Yalta)

My little actress,
                    The frail white birch
planted near my favorite seat
was split unluckily by lightning.
When the storm clouds gathered overhead,
the scarlet stars of pimpernel closed.
I watched the two cranes with clipped wings
start their odd waltz through the garden
and around the imported eucalyptus.
Then rain fell: one gray sheet of water
smearing my French window. The garden,
the row of peach and apricot trees,
and the spreading plums with fine red leaves,
looked like the waste of a ruined orchard.
I sat up writing and the rain slowed
until I could make out the details
of the small Japanese trees, the vines.
And the avenue of acacias
in the receding wind, bowed their tips
and drew back up again—restless
and disconsolate in their movements.
The long char on the birch's bleached bark
is ugly—a dark damp glimmering
in the last bit of evening light.
I am not well here without you.
The standard roses are unfortunate

in their beauty, the poplars in their size.
One of the squawking cranes cannot be found.
Someday this long stand of trees will seem
audience enough, and the slight breeze
lifting through the tangle of branches
will endure easily like sadness
or the subtle disappointment felt
after good weather or lovemaking.
The tree may survive. It's hard to say.
Someday. I hope to see you soon.

ON THE WAY TO SINGAPORE

This kind of fear is not new to me.
One night on the inland trip, I woke
to a breeze of dust and mosquitoes.
The moon, liquid and turquoise, reflecting
on the surface of Lake Baikal,
lit the tall grass along the paths
the reindeer sleighs cut into the woods.
I had heard such paths into the forest
when overgrown at the end of spring
might lead to an illegal still
or the encampment of escaped convicts.
I searched for a long while in my bag
for a pocket-knife I swore I had packed
until I was tired again and slept.
Tonight it is easy to imagine
how dark the sea gets beneath the ship
and how carefully a weight might drift
to the soft silt and sediment.
I have to use a handkerchief
all the time, now my cough has begun.
In the evenings I feel feverish.
We have buried two bodies at sea.
When you see a corpse sewn in canvas
hurtled with a slow somersault
into the water behind the stern
and when you remember just how deep
the water grows beneath the ship,

you begin to feel afraid,
and you have the idea that you too
will die and be thrown into the sea.

READING IN BED

Chekhov writes of a man
who loved gooseberries so much
that little else mattered.
His devotion was simple,
complete, yet involved loss,
the way the lack of foliage
in the midst of winter
allows the mind to imagine
the abstraction of a line.
In the story, as now, a sudden rain
taps the window.
As we both sit up reading tonight,
the light from our individual lamps
sets us apart,
the room somehow larger
in the evening's diminishing clarity.
Months from now I will remember
everything I did not say tonight
—how it is possible to love,
how the air at the beginning
of any season smells the same,
the sky different
only in the number of birds
cutting the frail arc of blue . . .
Once I believed that in touching
there was a language that outlives loss.
But now, as you turn out your light,

I am glad I have said nothing
and have instead lived
in another's story for a short while.
I could say I am happy
but I know what I am feeling
is no more permanent
than the narrowness of a road
where it becomes a point on the horizon,
and if I walked down that road
the trees on either side
would grow larger and separate,
detailed, though bare.

RETURNING IN WINTER

after Czeslaw Milosz

Think what you will about this place where we have
come—the light settled on gray silt, the creekbed
choked with leaves, a fine mud, the clay of the bank
tumbling in.

I cannot remember myself here before, now that it is
winter and the snow begins to fall.

The paths are empty, smooth where no one has walked.
Soon, eroded gullies will be drifted full of snow.

I could believe that without wind the tall dried grass
would continue to lean away.

I could believe that in summer vines tangle around
the unkept hedges, the red thorns and ripened berries
lining the thin green limbs.

I could believe that, yes, I lived here once with you,
instructed by nothing I would know enough to remem-
ber. I pull my coat around me and listen. There is the
cold, the ice creaking in the trees. The clear sound of
the world beyond forgiveness.

We were so wise then. We believed cruelty was weather,
and could change.

REASONS OF ICE

The house sits up ahead on the hill
—the roof white, weighted with a whole month's fall.
It's quiet here. There's no sound
from the schoolyard or from the owl
whose wing shadow looks like a blue blade
against the birch. Even as the owl
falls into flight, there's only my breathing.
Today, old snow grays in the ditchbank.
Spruces shagged in hoods of frost.
And the owl, in its one beauty,
is a thing I cannot touch.
I would like to hold this still world,
if the world were a thing to be held.
But it's here beneath me, solid,
with the same punctual cold.

I was surprised when I walked out this morning
by the suddenness of light, silver
on the mountain laurel's green—a color out of place
above the snow's sooty tatterings.
I must have been looking for something
—something that would survive this ice,
its sheathing. All I am left with now
is detail: the birch mottled with lichen,
the rust and yellow-white of ground cover,
the Christmas fern's thin shuddering
beneath the sag of hemlock.

It seems, now, there is nothing beautiful
about the owl as it settles
upon an oak's stiff limb,
nothing beautiful about its patience,

its eyes, in shade, darker than mud,
its large fist of a head cowlicked.

FOR THE NEW YEAR

for Jennifer

White walls kept white, rubbed with chalk

and limewater. The sun, now,
released from behind storm clouds

is opening somehow—white
upon the winter water.

The whole house skirted with snow.

Snow fills the bamboo basket.
One straw-colored sparrow flits.

A dusk-brown deer, flecked with white,
nudges the round tufts of moss.

The yellow of pine needles.
Yes, these are generous days.

The duck marinates in dry
red wine. Stuffed with potatoes,

one recipe says, or fresh
cranberries and wild rice,

it is a holiday meal.
Although the flesh is dark

and sometimes slightly bitter.

Once, on a stalled bus, in March,
I woke to a child's soft voice

explaining, "No, Mom, you're wrong.
You shouldn't draw it like that!

A heart looks more like a fist."

Rose hips seen from iced windows.

The taste of mollusk. Mushrooms
cooked in garlic and butter.

The still cold brought in on coats.
Nothing's sad about darkness.

The clear dark of cabernet.

This is what I wanted most:

the snow revealing itself,
the slow kind laughter of friends,

a dust of frost, a morning's
tender dull blue arriving.

This light after the body's
pleasure. Always this light.

A WALK WITH MY FATHER

A columbine's clear violet after noon rain.

The ditch of a creek we'd followed here,
muddy water stippled with shadow. It is 1966.
On the bank, a carp, or what was left of one,

covered with a glow of flies. Green, gold,
a momentary body of light
lifted as he turned the fish over with a stick.

The exposed flesh was flat, white,
raw as wound. Unearthly.
Or too much of the earth:

the dull texture of clay, the dust white of lime.

To satisfy me, he pushed it over the grassy bank.
The heat was visible on the rank air,
rising against a drift of daisies.

I followed the fish downstream until it caught on rocks
—pale jutted limestone, and the slow water
worked its gill. Opening, open, as if that would help.

TORNADO WEATHER

This evening in the settling dark,
in what my father called tornado weather,
I watch the heat lift its shimmering weight
above the snapdragons and low sumac
into what light remains inside the maples.

Those long nights while I was up,
sick, heavy with heat and dreams,
I was sure it was my father's broad palm
pressed against my forehead
that held the fever in.

I am no better without him.
If the dark brings with it relief, a chill,
it is a trick—weather storing up its storm.
June bugs rattle the screen, annoying as ever,
like the song he murmured that would not let me sleep.

THE HORSE

The horse my mother sits on is pocked
with dry red clay from the gully.
And as always, the horse will fall

when the five o'clock whistle blows,
when the light glints off the rusted roof
and workers leave the cannery.

Today she is fifteen years old.
She is cool in her cotton dress.
The horse breathes beneath her slowly.

The worn stirrups dangle empty.
Brown chestnut oaks creak in the wind.
Above hills rutted with erosion

a horse buckles beneath its weight.
It lands with a thud against rock.
The hull of its body. The air,

hot and damp within its shape, forced out.

I have chased it here to this pond,
or what was once a pond, but now,
in the dry season is a marsh.

The one shot muffled to a clap
cracks the horse's hard-boned forehead.
It sinks into the gray-green ooze,

the mud grows up its side like mange.
The blood like oil on water.
At dusk, only its head remains

above the surface, black, outlined
with faint scribblings of moonlight.
It's my duty to watch the horse

until its eyes are covered and
the last bit of air escapes its lungs,
until it's irretrievable,

until someone comes to relieve me.

In a borrowed car's torn back seat,
mother's brother sits with a gun
pressed against the roof of his mouth.

Beyond the hills of white maple
evening is rehearsing itself.
And with a click night replaces

the farm machinery, the horse
rotting in the renderer's truck,
the lovers parked along the road.

With a click the rear window burns
like a ditch full of wild flowers,
a deep blue red against darkness.

My mother waits on the roadside,
lit up white by the two headlights.
Sweat makes the soiled dress cling to her.

The only thing she can do is wait.

Heartwood (1988)

CRAB APPLE

The thin chipped branches of the crab apples,
    are as hard as anything
  that holds on beneath the iron cast
    of late autumn sky.

Whoever planted them as ornament
    must have loved the scattered nest,
  the broken-knuckled look of the thing,
    must have loved the fruit,

the unripe pithy white, the dusty red,
    some speckled with mold, some pecked
  but not eaten, the holes edged with black,
    black like charred paper.

If the trees are bent it is not from fruit.
    Each year they shrink a little.
  The ground beneath them goes soft with rot.
    The bark grays like shale.

You can only eat so much sour jam,
    and when you do you are left
  with the cramped, twisted look of the trees,
    a look so jagged,

you almost forget the season they flower.

THE ROAD TO EMMAUS

This is what they are offered. Their bodies, their eyes
      which fail
them. It is springtime. There is rain and the paths are
      rutted.

The gray mud along the road is a gravelly mortar.
There is an apple tree among the trees of the wood, light

in the rain-white smoke of blossoms. This is not suffering.
This is the story of what suffices, how the body

can be divided infinitely, how it can be held
like bread in the hands of a stranger, bread which is
      broken,

the dust of flour falling through the column of sunlight,
dust so finely lit it becomes nothing before their eyes.

DEBTOR OF HAPPINESS

Whatever empties the feeder
comes and goes without my knowing.
There is little satisfaction
in their names or the songs I've stopped
listening for. The birds that come
come in spite of me, are welcome
to rule the yard and its one tree,
to pick and scavenge the little
I've left them. I stood among them
once. The morning after Halloween
I broke open a frozen pumpkin
against the trunk of the maple
and chickadees and cardinals
and even a cedar waxwing
cleaned out the three jagged fragments
of their hard white seeds. Once I walked
along a river's marshy bank
pulling a canoe through the shallows
and all the sounds were water sounds:
the reeds swayed by wind, the wet call
of the killdeer, the heron's blue stealth.
Above the quick cut bank, sparrows
broke the air into flight like rain.

I believe the birds no longer
sing their one song of alliance.
If the hummingbird works its way

through the damp dust of evening,
if the black sweep of a crow's wing
or the jay's miserable crying
sends the other birds scattering
I am unaware. I feel the earth's
pull and cannot even look up
to see the nests in the winter limbs
or the hawk circle its hunger
above the rain-washed riverbeds.
Now in my dreams if I fly
flight is more like a falling.
I used to wake to their songs once.
I would listen and I would hear.
It was that simple. What I heard
wove a wreath in the air. I lived
beneath it like a happy man,
as if there were nothing, nothing but air.

NATURAL HISTORY

1.
Light settled in slowly like silt in the choked-off creekbed
until morning. Time passed like that.

After a long hunt for fossils in the scarped and silvery
clay of the bank

my brother couldn't decide
if the chipped finger-length stones we found

were the remains of marsh grass, or the spines of extinct fish
that lived so deep they were their own source of light.

But everything, he told me again and again, was turned
in time to calcium.

Pith or marrow. It didn't matter. He knew such truth.
He knew that sinkhole,

collared in black moss, where we sat listening to the deep
water's echo hollow in the distance,

might have been the bottom of the ocean.
He knew that the rise our house was built on

might have been a tidal island or a reef.
He knew that after the water receded, there was ice

and that wasn't the end of things. That's years ago,
he told me, before you can imagine.

2.
Summer nights, the grass not yet damp, we lay on our backs
and let the world, everything that held us down,

take us with it. The sky, each star locked in place, turning.
The heavens, we called it.

A machine we dreamed we invented,
so fragile it might break at our touch.

One night, after a week knotted with high winds, tornadoes,
we watched the clouds pile up,

the known dark above us collapse into blackness.
We believed God was up there, hidden. The rain broke

so suddenly we were soaked
before we could get to our feet.

Quick with lightning,
the rain and night flashed a moment of white.

That's what He looks like,
my brother said as we made our way to the porch.

Just like that.
Another stroke backed by thunder halved the changing
     dark.

We laughed, uneasy, our eyes blinded
as if we had seen Him. Just like that.

OVERCOAT

The day my father came home, blood still wet
on his beige overcoat, the gash broken
open across his nose, raw and steaming
as he entered the house, it was Christmas Eve.

"I put the car in a ditch," was all he said
as he raised his hand to touch his wound, but didn't.
He was half-drunk and stood there like a child
needing help with the buttons on his coat.

I remember the water and soap, my hands
rubbed red as I worked the heavy fabric,
but the stain held fast, a splotch of brown
like mud outside where rain had worn away the snow.

Slumped on the couch, he talked himself through his sleep.
And as he slept, I drove from store to store
looking for the exact coat and when I bought it
I didn't have it wrapped. I even thought

of putting it on and stopping somewhere
to get dead drunk for the first time. I didn't.
He was half-drunk, which meant he'd wake easily
the next morning and remember enough

not to say a thing. He'd wake with crusted blood
along the ridge of his nose, with his coat
thrown over him as a cover and know
I'd given it to him and that it was not a gift.

WITHIN A CIRCLE OF RAIN, MY FATHER

He waited for a light
that might save him. Gray,
the day spread from salmon
to gray. The dawn damp smoke,

the sky tipped and spilling
dark from the center, dark
blotting the far torn edge
until the whole day burned

whole. The static of rain
like scratches that shiver
white at a film's end, then
white fills up the blank screen,

that rain surrounding him
was the end of something.
And he could see the lace
which was the beginning

of light through the blue shreds
of his private circle
of rain. He could see light
sway the green-stemmed brush

and drift of bridal veil,
light catch on the ant-traced
buds of the peony.
That rain surrounding him

was the end of something.
As he moved to the light,
light that would have saved him,
rain filled in the spaces.

SNOW ON ASH WEDNESDAY

I was lazy last autumn;
I let the garden go wild,
let it fall in upon itself.
Now networks of stain hold on
like shadow to the white wall
of the shed where tomato
vines, fragile from winter,
crumble off the string lattice.
This morning near Saint Mary's
I watched slow heavy snowflakes
spiral down the chalk gray sky
and when the wind shot between
the church and parsonage
the column of snow shattered.
Flakes flew up like ash over smoke.
Ash is what I saw today
on the foreheads of children
who made snowballs on the steps.
Their mothers lingered and talked
beneath the high arched doorway.
The children waged their small war.
One boy, caught upside the head
by a throw, began to cry.
The charred cross above his eyes,
smudged, unrecognizable,
ran in dirty streaks along
his nose and onto his cheeks.

Above it all, pigeons chirred,
hidden in cornice shadow.
I expected the mothers
to be alarmed, or the birds
to lift from their white basin
of snow with a dull flutter.
But the boy just cried, his hands
soiled with his blessing.
I could do nothing for him.
Now the snow has turned to fine
cold rain. What remains unwashed
remains—all I am left with.
And that boy is no better
for his pain, for what he lost,
with his hard face in his hands,
tasting it all—salt, ash, ice—
what wears away at the world.

METAPHOR

To capture the morning
   along the washed-out town road
above a slope too steep to grow crops
   he shoveled up this tangle
      of weeds and grasses—

each separate, clustered:
   feathery shoots of yarrow,
dandelion florets closed tight above
   their jagged damp leaves, cocksfoot,
      spare spikes of heath, rush

and fleshy plantain.
   He carried it home before
the dew dried, before the green mass grown
   heavy with itself wilted.
      The sod in his hands

was wet and ragged
   with white tubers and nerve-like
roots. The dirt sifted through his hands
   fell in a trail behind him.
      Posed at eye-level

on a shelf above
   his table the square of earth
grew richer as he painted—
   creeping Charlie, meadow grass,
      clear for the first time

as the light, which was
   by now water and color,
dried still and permanent on paper.
   Springtime held in check, steadfast.
      A cool wash of green.

A study, he called
   it later. An exercise
toward some greater painting. Perhaps
   the wild growth among the rocks
      of Calvary hill,

or beneath the head
   of a waking guard surprised
by light from a tomb that bright morning
   when spring arrived forever.
      In this old story

about a painting,
   in this long meditation
there is another, unknown story
   about the young apprentice
      who mumbled and bitched

as again he swept
   the floor after his master
tracked in the red-clay soil, the straw
   thrown down outside the doorstep.
      When the boy stopped work

long enough to say
  he had had enough, he quit,
the artist did not look up, did not
  take his eyes off the green clump
   losing its luster.

The boy cared nothing
  for a mess of weeds, for years
of calculating the pure proportion
  of head to hand to body,
   the raw stink of oil.

Although his trained hands
  were skilled enough to copy
Christ's passion, a body in torture . . . ,
  he cared nothing for beauty.
   He wanted to be

a soldier, wanted
  to feel the taut right angle
of a bow string as he released it
  shimmer into music.
   He wanted to go

to the Promised Land.
  So he gave up sweeping
and walked out into the clearing day.
  He walked the rutted roadway
   pocked with black puddles

south away from town.
   The old man could have his weeds,
he thought, stopping by the embankment
   from which the sod had been cut.
      It looked like what it

      was—a scar of mud,
         not a grave's first shovelful
torn away. He did not believe in
   metaphor enough to see
      it as that, a grave.

FAMILY MATTERS

Drunk, she held her first granddaughter.
The woman swayed and laughed, lifted the child up

at arm's length above her head. When she fell
she fell in the slow motion in which all

accidents happen. Her son, who had just
entered the bedroom, caught his mother

around the waist, still he, the baby
and mother toppled together

onto the unmade safety of the bed.
In the end it was not the baby

he thought about—the baby would be fine—
but how he had to lift himself out between

his mother's legs like a man.

OVER HIS SLEEPING AND HIS WAKING

Here, he thinks was a kingdom. The leaf he crushes
crumbles into dust, woody threads and hard edges.

And the wind that scatters it is the same old wind
that blew before the ruining, that blew over

everything. Over his sleeping and his waking.
What was once a kingdom. Once he believed it all

his own. Each day and night a landmark on a map.
What he had forgotten was like a washed-out road.

Here—beside the splitting trunk of a Chinese elm,
its line of hard bark and wound sap, its weight pulling

itself in two, the skirt of leaves and damp plowed earth
of the earth and grub worm—here, he thinks, I begin.

IF YOU CAN

for Clare

In your life you will bruise your heel.
You will be walking some day and step
down hard on a sharp rock.

Whether you cry or curse or just feel
pain shiver up your leg, you will take
your next step with more care.

You waited a long time to be born.
We waited with you, waited for you
in this world full of rocks.

Once I believed I was saved, beyond
the trouble my family, my friends
and my own stupid choice

brought me. But saved by whom or for what
I don't know. But somehow I was.
If you can, please, believe.

It does not make the rocks any less
hard. It is not like ice which fills cracks
and shatters rocks into dust.

But it makes you feel a tenderness,
like blood cushioning the hurt, a bruise.
It shows us where the pain is.

Apocrypha (1991)

PRAYER

What then but to give in,
Having felt the rush of the fugitive
Released as easily as a breath,
Having been burnished like beach glass,
Crushed and left whole,
Between spirit, between spear point
And forge? What then but rage
That when spent rages
As dogged surrender? Sweet,
Sweet anchor, how long
Your hook held.

NOCTURNE

Soon enough night will have its dominion.
For now surfaces abide. The pink
Blooms and shadows on the tidal flood
And the full sanctuary of the salt marsh
Beneath this sky persist and thus rescind
The worn urgency of the early moon.

He walks awhile, and senses still
The rank wreckage of the low tide.
Smeared reflections double the moored hulls.
Asparagus, head-high and feathery,
Otherworldly in its bluish lace,
Sways against the stiffness of marsh grass.

He walks awhile among these shades.
Dusk is this round water, this uneven ground.

AT DUMMERSTON BRIDGE

It's not the bridge crossing the river,

But what is half-seen beyond it

—Viridescence, what she knows is forest,
The air gin and pitch, the shade
Of the understory and ledged bank—

That divines the night to come.

The stars are scrimshaw and the dusk
Warm with a hurry of blurred lights.

The whippoorwill echoes its name,

A compensatory music for one
Who is drawn to it, for one called back.

PROVISION

Between a laugh and rare luck
A man makes provision for clarity.
He is the beholder who holds little:
The moon, what is left of it, reflected light
Drawn as the expression of full knowledge,
Another day's spent endowment.
As in the cold world, the sheltered world,

The air of earth and foundation,
The example overshadows the argument
And is illumination: a cast, a casting.
Clarity is not precision, the particular
Intersection, the crude X.
It is what the tools cannot measure:
The gap, the lack, the verge of arrival.

SORTILEGE

Contact and intersection, a communion
    With the unrisen moon
Troubles the sharp doubt that delves and disciplines
    His labor and purpose.

How level and cutting the flight of swallows,
    Their brusque discord at dusk
And flood tide, when the momentary fixity
    Of fullness ends the day.

Prophecy takes the shape of interruption,
    Irritability,
The withheld. He opens a book at random
    And consults randomness.

THE CONTINUANCE

Now that the day is adjourned, he returns
To routine devotion, to a knotted rosary
That is nothing more than a calendar,
The cadence and creep of a kingdom come.

It is hard to know from the evidence
If a judgment can ever be made,
If he is the one to hand down a verdict,
Or the one who stands, when asked, to hear his fate.

The herb garden, green through the warm winter,
Has been scoured by an abrupt ice storm.
The mint has gone from flower to char,
Yet by his effort (the old sheets thrown over

The garden bed each dusk) the leafless sticks
Stand in their rectitude, and the patterns—
The braids, the knots, the compass—although torn
And skeletal, suggest their once-full form.

Long ago he cut back the roses.
The earth, mounded out of necessity
Around each, is too easily compared.
A pile of dirt remains a pile of dirt.

APOCRYPHA

One argued that the manuscript
Could not be authentic. It lacked spirit.

One stressed that the word they'd translated
As *earth* should be, in fact, *clay.*

Another agreed that such attention
Was important, but at this time deviated
From the intent of their inquest.

Soon they forgot the fragmented scripture
As each interrupted the other.

The one standing column, which stood
At the edge of what they believed
To be the edge of the city,

Counted the hours. Its shadow
Lengthened and shortened and lengthened.

THE MAP

               The horseshoe lake
Has been reclaimed by the river. Woods,
Represented by a flawless wash
Of green, were cut, burned, taken
By insects or disease—he could not
Remember and perhaps each was true.

His duty was to draw the map, to pay
Attention to the landscape's details
—Each strategic cliff and pass—to mark
Disputed borders with a broken line.
Still, by the time he finished his work,
By the time messengers and armies

Followed the unpaved road, which followed
The long blue stroke of river, the map
Was obsolete. Few returned and those
Who did could tell him little that helped.
If they talked, they talked of casualties.
No one had reached the edge of the map.

There, for all he knew, the green, vine-like
Branches rising out of a tree stump
Tangled a knot around an axe.
A warm wind moving along the tips
Of the cypresses shuddered like fire
Down the rocky hills to the ocean,

If at the end of land there is ocean.

52

ICON

Where the blue paint has cracked and chipped
Away from the Madonna's skirt,

Wood, worn by hands that have lifted
The figure through the streets each year,

Shows. A palm's worth of exposed wood,
Rubbed smooth by the salts and oils

Of touch, burns warm in the stammer
And stammering of candlelight.

She looks down as if not to see
What large presence looms above her.

And if she could see she would see,
As revealed through a tear, her flesh,

A slight curve where her hip would be,
Where even the hand of a god

Might rest after he covered her
With touch, where the men, who could not

Help think that it was immodest,
Took hold and hoisted her above them.

PALM SUNDAY

Three weeks ago forsythia rattled its sticks.
Now, though not an answer, not a reprieve,
The redbud flowers from its hard black trunk
And the magnolia rocks in the wind,

An ark that carries only whiteness and blush.
The dogwood's limbs have not revealed their bracts'
Stigmata, and for that she is thankful.
Why does He descend into the city,

She wonders each year, into History,
His advance raising up dust, a figure
Of dust, which is each of us following
Him? Dust the wind easily disperses?

And why do we repeat the meager fanfare,
The palm leaves bidding welcome and farewell?
She descends the church stairs and does what she must.
She hurries home to the life that's hers.

Each year she looks out for an answer and finds
Only spring's unmiraculous onslaught.

WHEN THE WOOD IS GREEN

The ample day hesitates, and that brief delay,
That tear in the momentum, that pause,
Is, for one moment, consolation.

But for whom? At this station, at this stop,
It is easy to see the crude shambles
A sequence of events can lead to.

Consider the ox pulling a cart full
Of spectators. It does not hear their jeers.
It does not decipher each rut that rocks the cart.

It knows the unbending shape of the yoke,
The shape it works against toward some end.

DIPTYCH

I had looked through these two windows so long
That what shade blocked and what light whelmed
Glared, then grayed, declined durably, darkly,
Until the frame of a diptych remained.
Only a frame to divide suffering
From suffering, the uncertain from grace.
Where but in the worn world is there equity?
In van der Weyden, the Virgin and saint,

Slumped, yet delicate and kempt, seem less earthbound
Than the dead Christ, un-descended, un-risen.
For the mourned and the mourners, torture is figured
As a foregone expense. Who could believe,
I wonder, that we are conceived in love?
The anvil wears away at the sledge.
I can hear it out there—*dink, dink, dink*—a dark
Undappled, undivided by the maker's hand.

TENEBRAE

How can we doubters explain the midday dark
When such an elaborate system of spars
And crossbeams propped it up? Though scaffolded,
Dark fell like heavy canvas, slack, unfolded,
A weight no wind could alter, a torn mainsheet
Tenting the sinking deck. Underfoot
This land is a wreck of wheel ruts and gravel,
Crazed with aftermarks, a hill that levels
Here where the killing's done. His body, unbroken
And lifeless, tackled down under the open
Shadows, seems in their arms a drowned man's,
Except for the wash of blood on his feet and hands.
How can we believe his tomb will stand
Emptied, cenotaph to a god and man?

THE DEPOSITION

Dead weight in their embrace,
An accommodation,

A crude translation into the temporal,
The body becomes its form:

Battered and commonplace,
Flawed enough to be true.

They maneuver it clumsily, without grace,
The center of gravity

A fulcrum for their thoughts
As it's braced and lowered,

Commended to the turned earth before nightfall.
A form requires no faith.

Their doubt is faith in form.

THE ALLEGORY OF DOUBT

He looks to edges, even to the blur,
The disturbed choppy air of mirage
Because he knows when two surfaces meet

What he witnesses is influence,
Cause and effect. Once, each arch
Of the portico framed a scene:

The brunt and the burial, the crown
And the veil. Once, the driven nail
Divined the lines of incidence

But now, removed, leaves a gap
That separates what he knows
From what he knows, *this* from *that*.

As he turns to leave, he moves his hands
Along a doorframe. Puts one hand through.
Still rehearsing the rudiments of ontology.

THE PLUM ON THE SILL

The cold at its poles and blush
Of blue at its equator
Do not equal a planet.
Composed as an example,

As *object,* this inspired shadow,
This timorous flourishing,
This dimpled orb, does not move.
Violet and gold, the whole

Spectrum of a grackle's wing,
A static arpeggio,
The plum in its plumness sits.
The linear and mythic

In its presence veer and curve.
Put anywhere it stays put.

FOR LUCK

for José

You know for sure you are lucky.
Luck fills you like the shape of your breath.

Then one day as you are reading it leaves.
It lifts up like the shadow of wings,

With the clean ease of smoke on a cold day.
Your luck is gone. You watch it fly away

Over the tracks, beyond Providence Road
Until it is out of sight. Your luck is gone.

Still somehow you trust tenderness
And all its romance, the fine caress,

The salt on your hands wearing away what they touch.
That is not part of the story.

If I should die, you said in the prayer
You said each night. If I should die before I wake.

You woke and listened again to the bent apple tree,
To the wind work the sweet ache of its load,

To the wren and the air it shivered through.
Luck, like hope, is always hollow-boned. Always

There is an updraft to carry what it can.
What it cannot falls upon your head like a blessing.

FOOL'S GOLD

I was not the type to call forth angels,
But if I said there's a swallow rising as it banks
Over the white flat of the rail yards,
Tracing the long ellipse of its hunt,
You could believe me. I talked like that.
I looked to the birds for the perfection of geometry.
I waited for three stars to show up
In the graying sky above my house
To watch the right triangle they formed
Fill in with darkness, with all the true
Unilluminated points of that plane.
The contour of the hillside, the white explosions
Of lichen on a boulder, the worn-away roots:
I disallowed nothing and took solace in that.

Bits of shell, a chipped lace-like fan
Of sea fern, and the porous knuckles of coral
All cleaved, fossilized, to the limestone
Outcrop near my house, a thousand miles
From any ocean. History had gone
A long way without me. Against all warning
I looked straight into the eclipse, looked
Into the light-crowned circle of black
While others watched shadows through pinholes.

The land would rise and level away
From the river, a river silver

As it ran from shadow into sunlight,
A river so full of silt, I thought,
I might walk on it. I'm not talking
About miracles. The bank sloped
So long and gradually that the mud
And slow-moving trunk of water
Were nothing but rills and deltas, intricate
Markings I thought I might decipher.
Each stone in the rift was placed
As if a clue. If the water
Shifted a fistful of pyrite
Glimmering beneath the surface
That too was evidence of a language
I was just beginning to learn.

MILK GLASS

What was left to her she now leaves to me:
Milk glass, a near-flat bowl with fluted edges,
A trifle that sits on the sideboard

As her sole marker. Its blue translucence
Is translunary, an overcast:
Ice that has no ancestor in ember,

But is a source and receptacle of light,
This morning's light the blue of backlit clouds.
She claimed her inheritance, hiding the bowl

On the day of her mother's funeral
And taking it finally when she moved away.
A child's act of theft that imbued for her

The bowl with pricelessness.
And so her gift is a gift of contraband.
No one is left who could accuse her.

The bowl sits on the sideboard, its cold beauty
As welcome as frost on the window, hard frost
That daybreak will not melt away.

IN MEMORY

If the world is created from the Word,
What can I hear amid the noise of that one
Assertion and all that rattles and diminishes

In its wake: the mockingbird's trill and grate,
The sluice and overlap where the creek narrows,
The dragonfly needling through the humid air?

And what will I hear when words are no more?
I cannot hear you now, ash-that-you-are,
My beloved, who in your passion and error,

In what was your life gave life to me,
My life from the life of your blunt body
That is no more. If I believe that Christ

Is risen, why can't I believe that we too
Will be risen, rejoined, and relieved
Of the world's tug and the body's ballast?

We are asked to testify, to bear
Witness to what we have seen and heard,
And yet our hope is in the veiled and silenced.

I take comfort in your silence,
In the absence of the voice that voiced your pain.
The body apart from the spirit is dead

But that does not mean the spirit is dead.

ABSTRACTION

1.
The eyesore on the beach was torn down.
The charred half-rafter hanging over
The gutted, broken frame and rubble
Fell last, fell as it should have fallen,
Undercut by flames, unsupported,
First. In three swipes the crane's shovel drove
The house down and raised cold cinder smoke.
The seagulls, mewling their childlike cries,
Pulled themselves into lumbering flight,
Outward from the pilings and then back,
A haphazard, elliptical chart,
Outward from the pilings and then back.

2.
He wanted to know she wanted him.
He wanted her to want him, to know
She wanted him without his asking,
Without hinting or soliciting.
To be wanted was what he wanted.
The ruined formula of his want
Was that he wanted. How could he know
What influence, what small coercion
His expectation had on her want,
The purity of her missing want?
He believed it to be missing, although
In this somber farce, how could he know?

3.
This will be his home: the foundation,
The stairway, the framed-in walls open
For now on all sides. The rooms seem small,
The halls narrow, too narrow to pass
Through together. When the doors are hung,
Perhaps, when the drywall and clapboards
Are hammered into place, perhaps then
The space will not seem so closed. The plans
Denied limits: luminous white lines
Opened the field of blue they enclosed.
He prefers the abstract design to this:
A place to live, a room for each need.

SCAFFOLDING

They spent a long time on the temporary structure,
Until the edifice, framed by cross planks and ladders,
Seemed a graph of idealized details: the corbel's bent
Disfigured figure, the flawed soldering on the stained glass,
The spade-like spear points and stone crosses. The
        scaffolding's
Grid, wobbly underfoot, stood sturdy enough to last
The disassembly. Each stone marked for the
        reconstruction.
Each ornament heavy with its function and excess.
A lintel next to a gutter, a statue's domed niche
Sideways beside the cornerstone, seraphim and saints
In the quiet chaos before recongregation,
Set down for the time being in a jumble on tarps.

EXPULSION FROM THE GARDEN

So they learned to build tools.
All night spent working an edge
Onto a stone the day dulls.
Birth, weather, and leverage

Are their sciences, the work
Of their imaginations.
Trial and error (spear, hook,
Net) make up their creation.

How to cut a straight furrow.
How to tie a sling to hold
A child and still work the plow.
What to use now. What to hoard.

Whatever works. A broken
Axe must be mended. The stone
Wedged well into the socket,
Bound tight and, once again, honed.

There is always work to do.
The child to be comforted.
A night of dreams to get through
Before the day has even started.

ESCHATOLOGY

Candor and clamor at the end of things
Glares and rings in a grammar that gives
Each word its place through clairvoyance.

It is not the lure of a past, gray
In summer drizzle at its worst, the morning
Poised at the gate, not exile from that garden

That instills nostalgia and brooding,
But a belief that joy will come,
That joy is relief and not a homecoming.

Although each sign, each cruelty, each promise
Has led to *here,* the tick of the escapement
And steady lunge and pause of the second hand

Go on. The mockingbird's song and the lily,
Fragmented and fragrant, respectively, fill
The last days as they filled the first.

THE LATE ROMANCES (1997)

CONFESSION ON THE ISLAND

Bound to them in their bondage to me,
I was a slave to those I enslaved.
I split the tree that hived the honey,

But the swarm would not bequeath a taste.
I tied a knot that could not be slipped,
But the weather wore the ropes to threads.

There is no escape, no need to sound
The alarm. The harm I did I meant,
Even when I said I meant no harm.

Romance conceals a dark tragedy
Played out long before the play begins.
What good's revenge? It's a blade ground

And ground until it is a foil,
The good metal robbed for the point.
Here on this strange island forgiveness

Reigns. Each crime buffered by drollery
Seems only the mischief of children.
I've lived out my life in Eden

Believing it to be the World,
Believing I could reclaim the lost,
All that was forfeited to greed.

Yes, with my death I will pay my debt.
Like you, Spirit, I am indentured.
I am blessed you took pity on me.

THE PEAR AS ONE EXAMPLE

Light, the common denominator,
Does not conceive, but cloaks and covers,

And by wrapping reveals: the pick
Chips a sliver of ice, the wheat,

Shadow-swept by a storm front, glows gold;
The pear curves the lines the blinds let through.

Asked to name it, who would not say *pear*?
The plump and dimpled base, the blunt stem's

Woody accent, the green that is green.
He closes his eyes, closes his hand

Around the pear and says: This is it.
This I would know without metaphor.

But his touch rubs up the pear's perfume:
A hint of honey and magnolia,

Grape and almond. None of it the pear
But the otherness that is the pear.

And then his mind wanders to Eros:
Is it the unknown made intimate,

Or the known masked by light's flimsy veil?
When he opens his eyes to see

If what he holds is what he has held,
He holds what anyone would call a pear.

AUGUST FUGUE

Rain, the last rain of evening, falls,
Unframed by the dark. The sound
Of rain as it falls sounds to them as sleep

Sounds: undisturbed, a slow weight
That drives a pendulum, what they hear
As the constant, the not-listened-for:

The sound that is their sleep, the rain
That falls. Which is beyond them and which
Within? They live. They live in indifference

And around them the last rain of evening falls.
She stands in the dark framed by the door
And hears the rain, without measure,

Unbound and precise, and when she turns
He turns and they give in to sleep. The rain,
Steady, clean, incises its fine shape

Against the dark. No scrape, no scratch
Mars the fall, the single declarative
Of its hush. She turns. He turns.

The rain is the sound that is their sleep.

TULIP

1.
Worthy Sovereign of Pandemonium,
Let the sultans fall and turbans unravel.
Let the parrot be your emissary.

2.
Yes, beauty soothes, but what one marries
Is its reprimand and its ruin: the house
Vacant, the dairy cows sold for slaughter.

3.
Poetry, however, is not a flower.
Who would speculate on a frill of words,
Offer as dowry the turn of a phrase?

4.
The cup, which once held tumult, holds
Nothing holy or worth a holy war.
Lord of Farce, make this tilled dirt your altar.

DON GIOVANNI IN HELL

1. To the Reader

The owl and bell betray the hour.
This is my kingdom beyond boredom,
In which I am subject and object.

Desire requires a foretaste
Of loss. I require less and less.
Come, voyeur, be my guest. Rest assured

This is no apprenticeship in vice.
You see, there is no mastery, no
Perfection of corruption. Excess

Is excess. My own acquired taste.
Push your thumbs into the orange. Arrange
The bodies for ease of entry. Please

Yourself. Watch as the bruised flesh gives way.
Taste the salt as the slow writhing halts.
The perfume, the consuming sweetness

Never recedes. Like you I have needs,
But how to name them here where the same
Charred rose rises each day, how to act

Upon them? When the cobbles shift and sobs
From the catacombs enter your room,
Do you call that hell, my hypocrite?

Be my guest among this ghostless mass.
Here form blears and disowns its content.
Repentance is all there is to repent.

Pleasure? Pain? No. There is no measure.

2. *The Body*

The calipers pinch as they close on
This slack form, this vehicle of lust,
Still addled with use and so other.

What did I expect, my God, from you?
The resurrection of the body?
The adagio of nostalgia?

The wax, an oily ichor, spills down
The candle's length. I cannot not
Touch my finger to the hot liquid

And when it cools, I peel it away.
If only flesh were so easily
Disposed of. But I am bound to it

Like a worn horse to a whippletree.
Who will untie the leather harness?
Who will pull the pin from the clevis

And let me drag my burden away?

3. *Ode on a Beet*

It is no heart but may as well be:
A loamy sweetness and brilliant mess
Buoyant on the dark mass of its own

Element. From here the purplish
Greens grow unseen, grow bitterer
In the hot air of the days above,

The heat of days that I once ruled.
Boiled, then quartered upon my plate,
It corroborates how my palate,

Now scalded, concedes to the subtle.
O for a valentine of cherry.
For the sticky ripe and stony pit.

But for one of little appetite
This pauper's diet is all that's needed,
A bloody show to sate the gut and heart.

4. *The Nostalgia of Don Giovanni*

Lord, I miss the gamut of birdsong.
The dismal haze that mackled the dawn.
The dissembling and the impasse.

The curtsy. The penitent kiss.
I miss the child's tears. The lifted veil.
The bluish gold that veins fine marble.

I miss the refrain of refusals.
The firm *no.* The elaborate stalls.
The raised blush at the mention of sin.

I miss the face of each who gave in.
The bleached bodice in place but unstrung.
The host like a coin upon my tongue.

The *noli me tangere,* the *why?*
I have not forgotten each white lie.
The moan of pleasure. The muttered *amen.*

I was a ghost made flesh in women.

5. *Ode to a Zucchini*

O uncouth squash, what is one to do?
One can pick at dusk and find at dawn
A clutch of needless fruit hard on the lawn.

Such blunt lengths without delicacy.
Abundance when one has grown weary
Of the crop. What the gardeners say

Is true: there's no giving it away.
The zucchini is one of God's two
Practical jokes. You know the other:

Between my legs, my prodigal brother.

6. *The Proverbs of Don Giovanni*

Don't squander the kindling on green wood.
A fool mistakes the heart for the choke.
A touch is worth a well-rhymed ballad.

For the crab every way is sideways.
For the one flattered nothing is false.
Even a devil can sing the old hymns.

Abstinence has no true opposite.
A pillager needs no accountant.
Lust is a wasp's nest burned as a torch.

Each garden hosts a hooded serpent.
Patience is dross; stealth a vein of gold.
How many stings is the honey worth?

7. *Elegy for Leporello*

Better a winding sheet and stone vault
Than a ditch and shovel's worth of lime.
Or to be taken whole as I was,

Rudely and without ceremony,
My mortal body dragged through the long
Shrill aria of ever after,

Where harmony dissolves to plainsong,
And plainsong to a metallic drone
Like the blue-throated hummingbird's whir

And furious standstill. Sleep now
My beloved accomplice, my shill.
The charnel house is your galleon.

May forgiveness crown your pretty head.
I would kiss your mouth, my lost double,
If that would revive or redeem you.

(To what good did my kiss ever come?)
We lived as if we had shared a womb.
Breech and premature, I blocked the way

And thus I was plucked and you followed
Through the open wound *(wide was the wound)*.
Lost is the comfort of that live crib.

We were like the thieves who died with Christ,
Like two brothers in a parable:
Actors, allegorical figures,

Leporello, but standing for what?

8. *In Whose Image*

Mine is a treasure of little use:
A spilled universe of mustard seeds,
The tedium of anything goes.

There is time to be censured and rent,
Time for rust to reave the relics,
Time to envy God each he will take

As his bride, each he must then ravish.
I did what I could to mimic him,
The God of my own exegesis,

The God in whose image I am made.
For all his loving, he is a brute.
Grace, like a scythe, cuts what it cradles.

THE PILGRIMAGE OF MY FATHER'S GHOST

Halfway home, he comes to the field's edge:
Deadfall, goldenrod, a moulder of uncut hay,
A rose-thicket hedgerow skirting the verge,

And beyond it, a decline into a ditch
That part of the year fills as a creek,
The water slow, moving beneath a smirched

Surface of algae and islands of leaf rot,
And the rest of the year, this: a dry furrow,
A nest of roots beneath the shale outcrop,

The cutbank steep where the curve sharpens.
The crab apple on the other side shimmers
As frost catches dawn and the day opens.

Bent, buckled, a snarl of dead and green wood,
The tree, he knows, is the tree he planted
And left to the will of suckers and bindweed.

What he has forgotten is the way over,
And as he struggles through the tangled thorns,
The sun, still cold, consumes him like a fever.

TO CHRIST OUR LORD

A fire unhooks the snag
Of brambles. The seed crowns crack.
The rye grass, white traceries,
Shines and then crumbles to ash.
Only you would find comfort
In the habit of a vine,
In the smoke's bitter odor.
Soon a killing frost will check
The sap and the cricket cease
Its long deliberation.
The moon, a scrim of errors,
Will turn its back once again.
But you will not look away.
You love all things equally
And that is your flaw. Tell me,
What is love compared to shame?

BRIC-A-BRAC

Say that sin is a seed that mildewed
Or scorched still germinates and prospers.
Or say that the end is prepared for.
The overture worked its sly magic.
When a phrase is next heard, we know it
And are pleased as it turns, when it turns,
Slow and brooding. We begin here: Here
Amid the bric-a-brac. Here inside
Amid order and fidelity.
The Day of Judgment is a day
Nonetheless, filled with laundry, errands.
The story, the story goes, starts
In innocence. It is morning.
There's no path hacked yet through the thicket.

THE KINGDOM LIKENED TO A FIELD OF WEEDS

The green is not wheat, but mustard
That once sown flourishes to seed.
Wherever it falls, it takes hold.

The field, an indelible smear
Of darnel, thistle, and burdock,
Stinks of rank fullness and welter.

A swarm hovers like the wet smoke
Of an effigy set afire
And dragged across the brambled field.

Within its chirm and drone, crows turn.
The axle of the sun is locked.
No shade falls on the kingdom of weeds.

DETAIL FROM "THE LAMENTATION OVER THE DEAD CHRIST"

The final gift that each affords
Is grief—requisite, not kindred—
A dismal freight as dense as gold.

As a body borne to its tomb
Is carried, so too they lift up
Their pain and leave it here with him.

It weighs upon him like a cloth
Infused in oils and spices,
A rancid balm bitter with ruth.

But she holds him as in her womb.
Now dread, not wonder, tinctures awe.
Once. Once she was alive with him.

STUDY

The wind. All things touched by wind.

The laurel, the little lamps of the tulip tree.
The crow, the gleaming crow,
Withholds its one thorny note,

A note that can rip a seam
From the mildewed canvas of dusk.

In the margins there are angels:

Scumble and crosshatch,
A smudge where a wing lodges
Against an earthly body.

Each a hurried sketch,
There in the margins.

The wind. Windfall. All things touched.
The wind preening the ragged cedar.
The wind mustering dust and debris.

The eye of an angel
Like the eye of a hawk when the hood is lifted.

BORGO ANTICO

Nothing is mercurial above the midday shadows
Or sallow. Noon's indigenous, heat-quickened clarity

Suffuses the ochre plaster, the aquamarine apse
Of sky, the green and cream-colored hills skirting the city.

What we reap is never the soul's true resurrected form,
But this bare kernel, this whole life kept whole within a
        husk.

We live in the body because it is flesh and is passing.
We live in the body because it is what we have to give.

HOMAGE

1.
O my God, looming and rough-hewn,
Forge me with rage. If this is the purge
Ferret out and scald the cold grub
Burrowed in at my heart. Let havoc
Consume its nest and larder.
Let your gold cauter stanch the wound.

2.
Fall inviolate sledge, and be known.
Blast away the sawdust and matchwood,
The ash-fall and rusted filings.
Let mc be your wedge, let that edge
Gleam from use, burnished as it divides
The flawed from this hammerdressed world.

SANTO SPIRITO

Above the terra cotta roofs, swallows dart,
Stitching together the gathered dust of day.

At dawn, humidity hangs like a hive.
How surprised we are to find we live here,

Here within our bodies. The air, downswept,
Is fragrant: soot, sweat, spikes of lavender;

The unrestored light gold and aquamarine.
All is known and tenuous. Tenuous and known.

Bells. Then afterward, the quiet after bells.
Our bodies are not hidden, but revealed

Before the spirit of whom we are guests.
Revived, we hold each other and we rest.

TWO-PART INVENTION

One should not love the grackle for its song,
Nor the pine for its flora. If one must,
The anvil may as well be an altar
And the loom, the scaffolding of heaven.
The invention of perfection was The Fall.
Still, one longs for discord and accords the flaw

Dominion over the whole. The rarest wool
Is not sheared, but gathered from thickets and thorns.
The fox is not cousin to the foxglove,
But the fox has its hole and the crow its nest.
The crow and the grackle wear the thunder's rags.
If God is a word, then words sally us forth.

LINES IN MEMORY OF MY FATHER: PONTE SANTA TRINITÀ

Water tarnishes
Green and cinnabar
A slosh against gravel

A shrunken river
A narrow rift
A poor excuse

But reason enough
For the stone bridge
That holds me up

If I am to judge
Nothing before the time
Until the Lord comes

Who both will bring
To light the hidden things
Of darkness and will make

Manifest the counsels
Of the heart then
Let me wait here

As heartless as he accused
Crippled by stroke
One half of his body

Dragged the other half
Across the waiting room
Just to hold me

His right hand lugged his left
Up to my shoulder
And he leaned against me

The half-dead weight
Of his embrace
Causing me to step back

And lean closer
Stumble and buttress
Through the awkward dance

Both of us old
Before our time
And each blaming the other

A poor excuse
Is as good as you get
He'd say and true

Or not he said it
The spirit here
Is the river

Moving and still
Slow after weeks of heat
Or at its will

With flood it continues
Half-way through his life
He cried *my god*

And fell with a thud
To his bedroom floor
I'll stay here on this bridge

In a city of churches
And let Jesus
Bent over his brood

Hang as unredeemed
As any man strapped
To a body in pain

I can live with it
My father said
Meaning he'd rather not

IN ARCADIA

Half-buried in scrub and red poppies
And half-exhumed, the barren half-moon

Of the threshing floor, fissured and chipped,
Is bleached the white of lime, of the moon

Itself, full last night, instructed in light,
In chapters of light as wordless as

The owl's wing. Not yet noon, the sun hangs,
Worn and burnished from use, like a heart

Made of glare and ember. The mint spreads
Its mineral flame down the hillside.

Amid the green, the lizard's tongue flicks,
A Y of blood divining the air,

There and gone. There and gone. There.

ESSAYS ON A LEMON

1.
Violet shadow. A blur
That darkens where it touches
The curved outskirts of the real.

2.
Pine resin and basil. Thyme
And turned earth: no concoction
Counterfeits the prime of zest.

3.
From the lexicon of salt,
One word transfigures the sting,
The resonant hiss of the clear.

4.
What could mar the sun's surface?
Not bay, or the poppy seed's
Blue. O ripeness, O glare.

5.
The lemon reveals itself
Only in the rare dusk-light.
It only reveals itself.

MELANCHOLIA

Removed from its axle, the chipped grindstone,
A useless mass, leans against the wall.
Above, scales hang on a hook, balanced and empty.

Half the sand has slipped as time to the bottom.
The bell, unrung, will not be rung at the hour:
The plumb bob of its brass clapper unmoved,

The glinting lip unshimmered into music.
The moulding plane, handsaw, and scattered nails
Rest, idle, spoiled for want of occupation

At the brooding angel's feet. A mold of rust
Waits to pock the polished edges and points.
As if the practical text of her neglect,

The book, clasped shut on her lap, remains unread:
The pages never dog-eared, the spine unbroken.
If she could bring a single hope to light

And not cast it aside in the dull allure
Of twilight and moonlight that overshadows all,
If she could unfurl her wings and imagine flight,

And allow the thought of flight to rise up
Without the ballast of set squares and compasses,
Or the marble globe that has rolled onto the floor,

Then she might see that beyond the clutter and forms,
Beyond the unrendered distance into which she stares,
All one is ever given is *this* clutter, *these* forms,

That distance to arrange and in arranging change.

APPROACHING ACCADEMIA: A NOCTURNE

It gets dark while they talk.
The vaporetto, almost empty,
Crosses the water. Revs, then balks,

Bangs against the landing stage.
As a rope creaks taut, she stops
Midsentence: the smudged vestiges

Of balconies, alcoves, and arches
And the running lights, drawn like oxgall,
Marble on the canal's inverted *S*.

He sees for once what she sees,
And seeing it, as through her eyes,
Knows her heart, or so he believes.

The loose, unraveled braids of the wake
And opaque green of the flat surface
Are rubbed up argentine as dusk

Deepens the canal. Domes and spires,
A string of white party lights,
A bridge's underside, and belltowers

All blur on the water's reaches,
Unfurl and glissade from berth to berth,
As the slack rope unknots and releases.

PROSPERO STAYS HOME FROM CHURCH

What if he called a thousand miles *arrival*
And let an egret rip out the fog's hem?

What if he started over again, one stitch at a time?
The dawn, gray as a whetstone, is cold.

A mud dauber worries over its grotto
Anchored in the slate eaves. All work is patchwork.

The wine left open on the table has turned.
Out of muck, haze, and low tide mire,

A demiurge might muster the wherewithal
To shape a world. Maybe he'd need some straw.

Maybe an anvil. Spit and dust to make a slip.
An old Sabbath breaker, he'd never rest

Until he fashioned from his disregard
Both the keen edge of a pruning hook

And something duller, like a human heart.
Until he conceived from his furrowed brow

Bach, and therefore *The Art of the Fugue*.

FOR NOW

For now, he prefers *adagio* to *presto*.
The blue, resinous perfume of rosemary
To the magnolia's velvet buds.

Someday he will learn to abandon
The unsubtle harmonies
But for now his hands reach for the chords
He learned to hear long ago as music:
His right igniting the single torch flare
In the sky of a chiaroscuro nocturne,
His left raising Christ above the toppled guards,
Who sleep through heat lightning's rumble and static.

For now, content with the present tense,
Swept clean of what-might-have-been—
Rumors and misplaced documents—
He can almost swallow the grit of a cry
Balanced like a pearl on his tongue.

SWORN DEPOSITION

What he remembers holds like a slipknot,
So that whether the tide nudged in or out,

Or if black mud marbled the sand, or rain,
A downpour, lugged its weight through the pines,

Does not matter: each moment caught or released,
Each moment overlaid by the next, embossed,

Watermarked, is never whole but detail:
Happenstance, not incarnation; rubble,

Not ransom. No, he cannot distinguish
Truth from half-truth, the peck of a goodnight kiss

From seduction, the well-made original
From the restoration's flaws. He recalls

Halfway through his testimony the logic
By which he had hoped to proceed. A wreck

Is what he has made of this and will of that.
Loving the flesh but forgetting the pit,

He sinks his teeth in. If he could play the Fool
With overripe buffoonery and skill,

Remember to say what both conceals and cuts,
Advises and mocks, with love and bitter wit,

And not always reply in this taut tenor,
A player who is always an amateur,

His love of the act might increase more than love.
But he is under oath and must behave.

What he has forgotten he has forgotten.
The lees stirred up settle back to the bottom:

Dregs on dregs, varve on varve, the sediment
Becoming, over time, a firmament

On which the life he lives is enacted.
Read back his answer, he cannot retract it.

IN SIENA, PROSPERO RECONSIDERS
THE MARRIAGE AT CANA

All sleight-of-hand trails the dross and clutter
Of the unseen, clumsily like an anchor,
Barely concealing its means as it deceives.

What else can be made of signs and wonders
But close readings and a display of awe?
What is left when the waited-upon is fulfilled?

After the standoff Jesus conjures a trick.
Should such an act be enacted knowing
The *next* and the *next* will be demanded?

Of course, he one-ups himself, causes a fuss,
And the story plunges headlong to finale.
And then encore. Above, in the Sienese heat,

A pair of ravens patrols the parapet.
Washed linens flap on the clothesline.
A shadow bisects the curved blade of the Campo.

As if in confirmation of a miracle,
The twisted olive bears the wind's history,
A gnarl that hinders the brisk disorder,

Renders it as the unmoved here and now.
Skittish pigeons clatter up in the air.
Into shadow. Out of shadow. And then back down.

And no one, not even God, lifted a finger.

THE AUGURY OF PROSPERO

In the split-open breast of the lamb,
He fails to read the deity's will.
With his stick, he pokes at the carcass.

He nudges the wreckage of ribcage
Aside as if the Truth were concealed
In the sealed-off chambers of the heart,

In the intricacies of marrow
Or the maze and switchbacks of the bowels.
He sees what he always sees: the past,

The unattended moments festered,
Bloated with all that was left unsaid,
Images haunting abstract spaces.

He stares at the cracked shoulder socket
And parses out its function and flaw.
By the time he glosses each sinew,

He has butchered the sacrificed beast
And makes a feast of his misreading.

Cenotaph (2000)

SEE THAT MY GRAVE IS SWEPT CLEAN

Words are but an entrance, a door cut deep into cold clay.

I say, *A late sky flagged with jade; ice on the pear blossoms.*
I say, *A thrush of cinnabar in the lily's throat.*
Behind each assertion, each gambit, I could place a question
     mark.

Behind each question, a residue of longing, half-assuaged,
An argument of brine-edged light the moon, your stand-in,
     doles out,
Grain by grain. Behind each question, a hook blackened
     with rust.

Begin with a clay bank, a chill wind's insufflation.
Begin with thumbflint, a fever, some sticks to fire the kiln.
Are words but an entrance? *Words are but an entrance.*

THE KINGDOM OF GOD LIKENED TO A DEER CARCASS

What the crow abandons, worms relish.

If I stare long enough at these remains
I will imagine a kingdom undone:

Surveyed. Staked off. Limestone and ivory.
A cathedral built upon a temple.

This bone a buttress. That one a crossbeam.
Every altar stone bloodless and sun-bleached.

Every chapel floor swept clean by the wind.
For now, wind shudders the collapsing ribs,

Swirls up a mote of fur like milkweed silk,
And touches the ruin intricately.

What the wind forsakes, dogs will drag away.

DREAM LANDSCAPE WITH OLD BRICKYARD ROAD CREEK AND BLIND WILLIE JOHNSON

I have returned to the creek, to the current-scalloped sand,
The mud bank that gives and gives against onrush and
      backwash,

To the gust-cobbled surface sun-flecked with amber, the sky
As bright as icemelt, or blue, in deep shade, or buttermilk,

At times, more depth than surface, black as charred fircones,
      or rain,
Rain at night and a slide guitar troubling an old hymn

That I have no voice to sing, but still discern from the hush
Of water oaks and willows, the full reservoir of wind,

The nighthawk and the field mouse, a voice calling from
      the porch,
And having returned to the creek, to these oxbow shallows,

I wait, hell-bent, as one waits for Judgment Day, knowing
With one or two steps, he can ford the depth and distance
      home.

COLD SPRING BROOK

1.
How does light affirm in its passing,
Moving as it does, like this water
Toward its diffuse, estuarial edge,
Running tidal through the wide green range
Of wetland shallows, rose, and reedbrakes,
Fresh to salt: a merge, a convergence?
Bound as he is to *because* and *therefore,*
To the iteration of desire,
No knell, no toll can stay the hour.
The dark comes on. If *no* is the dark,
Should not light in its passing affirm?
To live in time is to be keelhauled,
Dragged and dragged beyond a single breath.
But breathe he must, so he breathes in.

2.
He builds the entire composition
Around an error—a sable-hair brush,
Slipped from his hand, salted Chinese white
Across a deep wash of ultramarine—
An error he hides by accentuation:
On all sides a thunderstorm's cordon,
Cold Spring Brook overfull at high tide,
A rain-stung gust across the causeway,
A dust slurry that mars the window.
The margins of what he surveys bleed

Into one green, one gray, one darkness:
His own reflection mere silhouette—
Featureless, suspended there, then effaced
Within the lightning-quickened instant.

3.
He has made of the narrow threshold
Between *landscape* and *contemplation*
An unlit altar where he augurs,
Where the thicket reads as a pathway,
Dusk as the dross of molten metal,
As blown smoke, driftwood's mineral ash,
Where memory becomes desire
Without alchemy or revelation,
Without the sediment of regret.
How indivisible the thing he meant
To render. Under his heart's crucible,
What remains unsaid waits as tinder—
Jackstraw and light wood—that will not catch,
Doused as it is by the cold, damp breeze.

4.
One June, after weeks of no rain,
The beach-edge of the marsh caught fire:
Wind lit the tall grass, wick after wick.

The stalks flared to filaments, cracked,
And sowed sparks to the ragged sand ledge.
Then the wind turned and a halfhearted rain
Haggled with what remained of the blaze.
By summer's end what damage there was
Was overgrown, a tangle of wild rose
Extending its claim on the low dunes.
In the time in between, he watched
The wide sickle of char glisten in rain,
Then green, consumed, as it had been by fire,
By a restless, wild welter, redeemed.

5.
It began as a sketch, and remains such,
Six or eight lines of charcoal dragged
Across the paper's tooth: the jetty,
The clapboard studio, copse of rose,
The Sound a flat expanse, an island
Where the white sky and white water fade
Into a boundary of early fog.
By habit, he troubles the page,
Reworks and overworks the surface:
Saw grass and heather here, a cedar edged
In shade there, until all is darkness,
A moment of morning cast as nocturne.
For once, he leaves well-enough alone,
Leaves the world, in its abstraction, true.

6.

The crow lives in the aftermath,
The osprey in the precarious *now*.
He lives somewhere in between, mistakes
The wreckage of his sin for punishment.
He knows only the sleepwalker's way,
The cartography of dusks and half-light,
The dull current from Deep River down.
And when he follows a line of thought
To its end, he finds a question mark.
How many questions can he yet ask
The proper answer to which is silence?
He stands at a threshold and looks out:
Night is a shadow box, a grave of silt,
A hollow that fills and fills with what falls.

7.

Say all of it can be taken back.
That each deed or word that worked its damage
Can be revised, withdrawn, stricken,
Ripped from the stained fabric of the moment,
From having-been-said, from having-been-done;
Say that forgiveness is not the issue,
But reparation. And afterward,
Forgetfulness, amnesia, the past
Showing no mark of the erasure,
No palimpsest of the act, the error. . . .
This is the lullaby that lulls him,

And as he falls asleep, the lines go slack,
Then tangle, voices in a little fugue,
A net that traps him under the surface.

8.
Oh, he half-sings. *The book of moonlight*
Is not yet written, nor half begun . . .
Until the words seem almost his own.
What a comfort a refrain when it returns—
The same words sung again, yet somehow changed.
He looks through his own reflection out
And calculates the distance between
The Old Saltworks Road and the horizon,
Between the horizon and all that curves
Away, unseen, and yet in its place.
What comfort a refrain when it returns.
He lets the window frame and arrange
The arranged world in which he is held.
Bound as he is, he lets the dark come on.

SACRED AND PROFANE LOVE

If it is indeed more fitting
To say that the world is an illusion,

Does it matter if what I behold is a gold braid
Inlaid upon ebony, or the wind-tousled jackstraw

Of salt hay that edges the marrow of the mudflats?
Does it matter if the gift the cicada leaves behind—

Hollow, dawn-enkindled, paper-thin—
Is the hieroglyph: *to begin again,*

Or the embodiment of cold light's sealed and sepia pallor
Beneath the ice floes of Europa?

In Titian's "Sacred and Profane Love,"
One woman is unclothed, exposed, and naked,

And the other is wrapped, decked, and bejeweled.
Each the image of the image of an idea.

Not an illusion, but an illustration.
Sometimes I can feel my heart in my throat.

Sometimes I can swallow nothing I put in my mouth.
What is a heart that consumes and is consumed?

HOW TO SUSTAIN THE VISIONARY MODE

Wherever possible, avoid predication: *the night sea, the dark river, this rain.*

As in a dream, where the door opens into a cedar grove, and the haze conjures a screen of sorts onto which an ill-spliced film is projected, and the words, poorly dubbed, seem mere trinkets in a magpie's nest, let each object be itself.

Objects a magpie might hoard.

:The blown dusk-smoke of flies above the sacrifice: The flames inlaid and lacquered: The horizon, a single graphite line on rice paper:

Revelation is and will remain the subject: "Behold, I come quickly: hold fast that which thou hast, that no man take thy crown."

The moment present and full: thyme-sweetened honey, a New World of Gold, quick with what made it.

Let distractedness be an isthmus connecting the day to day, dazed with the fume of poppies.

Let the daydream, dimmed by slow rain, skip like a shuttle through the loom's scaffolding.

Let the rain rain all day on the slate, a province of rain, gray as the stone no longer quarried in these hills, gray as the pigeons tucked in the eaves:

The rain, the dark river, this night sea.

HOMECOMING

In time, thunder unshackles the rain.
The tassels of pollen fall. Dust,

Not breath, becomes the spirit's habit,
A finery of grit that gathers.

The jay, a blue throb in the holly,
Will scold as it bolts. What exile

Would not love the evergreen for its thorns,
The bird for the objection it sustains?

CENOTAPH

1.

In the shallow domain of light's fitful flare,
An aviary of silt and minutiae drifts:
Pinpoints of citron, lilac, and sulfur,

Chips of shell-pink, a medusa's plume and ruff,
Coral cleaved and sundered, its dust offcast,
A constellation untied from its mooring.

How close the splintered sun that bracelets my wrist.
I reach down through to the edge of my seeing,
Beyond the fan vaulting of bladder wrack,

Through eel grass, through fallow shadow realms,
But I cannot pull you back to the surface,
You who are the body of my confession,
The cold weight of water that unearths a grave.

2.

How long did the crescent moon trawl in the wake?
How long before the wake itself collapsed?
Before *North* and *South* held the same compass point,

Marked the same unfathomable distance home?
The night above you is a capsized hull:
No air finds its way through the caulked seams.

Nothing can hold the body for long.
Burned by salt's caustic, ropes would frazzle
And a canvas shroud, rived and flayed,

Would let loose the dark matter of its cargo.
Thus I offer only provisional words:
Each a winding sheet of reef wind and whitewash,
Each a tattered disguise for the travesty.

3.
From a distilled essence of quartz and rose,
From a gramarye of psalms and waves,
From strewn stones and a hazel rod,

I have built this empty tomb for you.
Let its fretwork of shadows be your raiment.
Let thunder's phosphor light your way.

Grief is weightless and hard-shelled
Like a seed carried on an updraft,
A seed set down on hostile soil.

I have built this empty tomb for you,
Which the tide will bury and not exhume.
Sleep as silt sleeps in its dark fall and depth.
Sleep as silt sleeps in its dark fall and depth.

A NARRATIVE POEM

The story of a story is order over chaos.
What is not known, or not yet perceived, is made known.

I am the Alpha and the Omega, John writes near the close
Of his Apocalypse. And then the chapter ends *Amen.*

Drunk, asleep on the couch, my father mumbled long
       columns
Of numbers he could not make balance. The open ledger

On the table matched figure for figure his sober dream.
There was no miscalculation. The story they told was true.

If Omega *is less than or equal to one, the cosmos*
Expands forever. If Omega *exceeds one, the cosmos*

Holds enough mass to contract, to collapse in upon itself.
Amen we say in conclusion, meaning *verily, truly.*

What is not known, I tell myself in consolation, will be.
The story of a story is order over chaos.

COMES A TIME

There comes a time when you no longer believe the night and its one alibi, believe the snowlight in the orchard, the ice at the heart of the onion, the fever kindled by hummingbirds, the wind bruised by an angel's fall. There comes a time when the name you have called yourself in hope and lamentation—*I*—that charred wick, that ruined column that once held up the world, that incision that never quite healed—*I*—seems a makeshift marker for this body that sustained you. Did you believe the struck match purged the air you breathed? Did you believe you were ever poor, hungry for something more than the little that filled you day to day? *"I..."* you start to answer, *"I...,"* knowing there comes a time.

A CONFESSIONAL POEM

The story would not resolve itself for the telling.
It remained not clouded exactly, but dense—like
amber—with its own color and hardness, a surface and
depth that mimic each other: light enters and takes a
long time leaving, caught up in the sepia, the golds, the
pale yellow of the river willow's leaves, the fog having
lifted, but still remnant: the odor that rises from the
book as you open it, the dead language of fossils in a
jag of limestone, the honey on the blade as it's scraped
from the combs. The story, if he tried to tell it now,
would move *away* from the causal, like all matter, dark
and light, from the trauma of creation.

THE COLD WAR

My mother nods off. A lit cigarette
Elegant between her long fingers.
The arm of the divan riddled with burns.

Lightning, out of sync, preens the maple.

What is the square root of *yesterday?*
How do I solve for the door ajar?
There's no end to it, my father would say.

My mother nods off. A lit cigarette
Elegant between her long fingers.
The burns like islands on an oily sea,

The obsolete map of an archipelago
Where the Bomb was tested year after year.
There's no end to it, my father would say

And ask me to warm up his drink.
The unknown, the variable we call *it.*
Upholstery smoulders more than it flames.

Lightning, out of sync, preens the maple.

ELEGIAC VARIATIONS

for Larry Levis

1. Mood Indigo

Ahead of me the day ahead

As I come down out of the Blue Mountain
Pine ridge dogwood
                     a palimpsest of haze
A gully of cornflowers

Where is the pleasure of arrival
Now that the *then* has become *now*

All that remains of the western night

Is the coal and indigo
                     of a hawk's eyes
Coal and indigo and a grain of salt

And of the fog
                 one drop on each thorn

How far I have come to be only here

2. The Starling's Lullaby

Another day kindled and put out

Thus the crimped thread of smoke
Thus the ember motes that glint and fall

Thus the acrid aftertaste on my tongue
                              after so few words

The cedar's charred wand
The nettle bed's sloughed ash
The saltlight flint-gray on the marsh

It is hard to extinguish desire

All evening the starlings taunt
From the conflagration of the firethorn

What it burns it fuels with the soul

3. The Parable of the Vineyard

The moon
              its mouth sealed shut with wax
Maintains its vow of silence

Across a rain-washed range
Across the stripped vineyard

Across the blade of a pruning hook

Left to rust in a furrow
                    you follow your father home

How can one not mistake
Intensity for purity
Paradise for these ill-lit shambles

By now the dark fields are wild with rose
And the thistle worn to a crown

4. *Three Crows*

Three crows overthrow the canopy
And caw down in judgment

Still I count the streaks on the tulip

Cast the sun out of rust and haze

Compose and shape the landscape
By implication
                    fog on the creek
Shadow on the berry canes
Yes I have counted the crows
A trinity high in the pine

I was called but did not follow

I was called by name and did not follow

5. The Blues

How heavy the mortal body of Christ
Two angels hold half in the tomb
                              half out
On display for our pity
                    and for pity's sake

His face unrestored
                    a bluish blur and canvas weave

No pain no suffering to be read
As compensation as consolation for our own

Lord I just can't keep from crying sometimes
Lord I just can't keep from crying sometimes
When my heart's full of sorrow
When my eyes are filled with tears
Lord I just can't keep from crying sometimes

6. Study for Rain

Between cypress and olive
                              the shadow of rain
The rag ends of rain blown clear

It rained and the rain stopped
How few of our certainties
                              resemble the truth

Rushlight cloudlight a dull smoulder
The hive a cask of untuned static
A tinderbox of sparks

Between the cypress and olive
                              the footpath winds
Where the marble's worn water pools

Had God not made pale honey
I should have said this rain was sweeter

7. *Nocturne and Refrain*

Now you may have the final word

As the salt creek overflows with tide
As the cutbank's grasses drift heavy
Like a dragnet in the flooded marsh
As a heron lifts from the surface
Without noise without proclamation
Emblem of itself
                    Swallows wheel
Wheels within wheels over the wetland
A rope goes slack a rope is pulled taut
And below an anchor scuffs the silt

Now you may have the final word

8. Confronting the Oracle in Fiesole

Only a lizard to show the way

Little green flame through the ruins
A wordless scrawl and scuttle on the Etruscan wall

Only a lizard to find a foothold of shade

If from the earth we come
If to the earth we return
Then there is in the end
                    no digression
The one way home is the one way home

Green and quicksilver in the sepia shadows
Green and quicksilver
                    the lizard holds still for now

For now still it holds its tongue

DIVINATION AT CHAPMAN BEACH

I mention the light on Cold Spring Brook,
—Where at the bend it abides, the tide gone slack—

Dull as a drop of solder on a teapot
Or, as the fog lifted, clear as the fine grit

Of sandstone, raw sienna, and native umber,
And the light changes (or so I'll remember)—

Jade, a transparency of shadows,
Quicksilver at the edges, lampblack below—

And my hapless shorthand cannot keep up.
Thus, the teapot engenders a teacup,

And I read the configuration of leaves,
But seeing no sign of what I might believe,

Rinse it out in the sink. How the world began
I couldn't say, but no one was looking on.

What I mean to say has to do with the light,
How, though divided from the dark, it shifts

Mote by mote to the weight of its absence—
Unstable, volatile, a confluence—

Never seen, not even for a minute
As *itself*—a glint, a glister, wholly split

(A clock stopped at noontide, a gold nimbus,
A glare's unpied, undappled transplendence)

From the gloam of velvet, cross-hatch of charcoal,
Muddy wash, surface oil drawn to marble.

If the world were to begin at this moment,
Here, where the freshwater brook runs to salt,

God would behold a flat *S* of gray,
Not dovetail or pewter, but of the banks' own clay.

Then more blue than gray, like a nick in pewter,
Like a dove's blurred flight. Then a blue like water.

PROSPERO IN PURGATORY

Wind riffles the marsh from sodden salt hay
To kingfisher green, from lead to gold ether,
From shale to slate to amethyst and pearl.

Long ago he gave up explicating the changes.
The footnotes grew longer than the text:
Digressions hemmed by qualification,

Observations overwrought with afterthought.
A recording secretary, he keeps the minutes—
The narrow shoal of fog and first light,

The drag of black drizzle across the dunes,
The shingle of rocks reflected in the delft—
In a crabbed shorthand of his own making.

Sometimes he nods off and misses a gust.
Sometimes he gives in to sleep and as he sleeps
Satan raises up a straw-built citadel,

Reigns for a millennium and is toppled.
Sometimes he wakes to a light so white
It seems the whole world has calcified.

What he sees he sets down as if the truth.

TO A MAGPIE ON THE ROOF
OF THE MANGER

You hid each star but one in a shallow shadow box,
A relic-filled cabinet of curiosities,

And let the wind rifle the tinder. And let the wind
Refurbish the straw, the stalls, and the dovecote's niches.

What happens to a moment held captive, a moment
Torn away, ransacked from the dull continuum?

In your beak, you hold a marble in which the world—
Shrunken, drawn long, upside down—is as round as the
world

That deceives us with horizons and vanishing points,
The parallel rows of grapes that touch in the distance,

The *far away* where all is drawn together at last.
From here, I can even see myself in the marble—

Bent, distorted, the sky below me like a blue pit
Over which I hang headfirst, confused like the damned.

WITHOUT YOU

The water yields no distance to the oar.
Worn like a salt lick, the moon is consumed
At last. It gives up what it has to give.

Who will snuff the lamp swollen with glare?
Who will lift a fever's muslin and exhume
The thousand and one stories of my love?

The touch of your tongue was a voyage of wind-swells,
A swan's blurred and exquisite agitation,
Bloom on a briar, rain and wine on my lips.

Without you, hoarfrost silences the bells,
The low rafters of the Resurrection,
Not yet restored, molder behind canvas tarps.

Without you, the orchard is strewn with windfall.
Four walls and one burnt match are my hell.

SANDY POINT ROAD: AN ECLOGUE

Again the day begins: the hour like Galilee,
Both an instant in time and a map's coordinates

In which and on which I put faith. Three yellow jackets
Halo a glass of Jack Daniel's left out overnight.

The horizon—silvered, chalk-edged, figmental, level,
Depthless—attenuates the moment and fools the eye:

A thin repertoire of contrivances, a premise
Of edges, a line's repose between two blue-gray slabs.

Abstractus: dragged away. To abstract the landscape,
To be in it in exile. Again the day begins.

There is a path before me and I follow it. *Home?*
Yes, there is a path before me and I follow it.

LANDSCAPE AND SELF-PORTRAIT

Two notes and an interval of silence. *Not here*
It seems to say, calling attention to itself.

If it is true that truth is ever new, as now,
Then the mockingbird's eye is the vanishing point.

These lines, which will never intersect, appear to.
How easily we are fooled. That dull red palm-print

On the cave wall is not blood but iron oxide.
A hand. Not a heart. The pigment, of earth itself,

Held fast and holds. The image was the image at hand.

THE ANNIVERSARY

1.

The constellation Virgo harbors a black hole at its center, but tonight I see the moon, ordained, a basilica of salt, mouthing its one secret like a saw-whet owl, and all that might be culled, collected, and classified beneath it, named as a disposition of objects, as a taxonomy, an order, a genus, or subject matter, is smeared with this salvaged and chalk-dry light, this fine-grained and corrosive distillate, this heirloom dust that gathers on the pearl button of the glove, its little satin noose.

2.

When I said, "But tonight I see the moon," I did not tell the whole truth, for I have not even looked outside, but have relied on the conventions of memory, and with a word or two the moon, like a body under siege, wears thin outside my window, the moon forages in the attic, the moon is hauled up like a broken whetstone from a well, for that is what I do with a word or two: avoid scrutiny, avoid measuring the lead weight of my own heart.

So, what do you think?

Book Title:

Comments:

Can we quote you on that? ☐ yes ☐ no

Copper Canyon Press seeks to build the awareness of, appreciation of, and audience for a wide range of emerging and established American poets, as well as poetry in translation from many of the world's cultures, classical and contemporary. To receive our catalog, send us this postage-paid card or email your contact information to poetry@coppercanyonpress.org

NAME:

ADDRESS:

CITY:

STATE: ZIP:

EMAIL:

☐ Send me *Editor's Choice*, a bimonthly email of poems from forthcoming titles.

www.coppercanyonpress.org

COPPER CANYON PRESS
www.coppercanyonpress.org

BUSINESS REPLY MAIL

FIRST-CLASS MAIL   PERMIT NO. 43   PORT TOWNSEND WA

POSTAGE WILL BE PAID BY ADDRESSEE

Copper Canyon Press
PO Box 271
Port Townsend, WA 98368-9931

ORACLE FIGURES (2003)

THE RECONSTRUCTION OF THE
FICTIVE SPACE

I open my eyes and a season passes:
A single moth wing shudders on the sill.
The gate cannot open into the overgrown grass.

But the way, lit by foxfire and firefly,
By the flint-flash of grit at the pearl's heart,
Is a past words cannot return to history,

To what the swallows inscribe on the air,
And here, on the outskirts of memory,
I look off again into that distance,

As if into a future, the lightning opening
Before my eyes like Scripture.
The equation at hand can be proven

By the spiral descent of the fishhawk,
By the curve of a tiger-lily's stalk.
Yet all I see is surface glare,

An afterlife of the afterimage.

ORACLE FIGURES

The soul is honey.
So say the fox tracks along the sandbank
Wind will smudge and rain efface.

I thought I could see the future,
But when I looked I saw the past:

Tied with a shoestring
And shelved on its side.
The binding's glue consumed by silverfish.

There is that moment
In the quarried dark of late winter
When a word begins to adhere to its object.

That moment, as all moments, is transitory.

In the garden of hours:
The thorn hour,
The husk hour,
The clove hour.

I waited for the wolf to devour the god,
To shake its head and scatter the bones,
To lap from the skull fermented honey.

150

Instead, fever,
Four humors fretted into a flame,
Ravened me.

My body a script
Read beneath the shadow lace of leaves,
Beneath the single grain of light the moon allotted.

The stars seen through the wire grid of the cage
Are what they are, and the cold, a dead language.
The depth of field and the field of vision, the dream
And its driftage, the dark's one garment dragged
Through the distant olive, are scribbled and hatched.
Doubt is part of the process of inquiry,
As is the single star downcast. As is the cricket.
As is the grass. As is the milk on a lynx's tongue.

Another constellation tilts into place.
The mesh of gears a hush I hear
As wind in the cypresses, wind in the ruins.

Each sentence I start to utter begins,
Once . . .
But all I find is a washed-out road.

Had there been a maple leaf
On the path, I would have picked it up
And saved it in this notebook

Between pages of words for *this* and *that*.
The moon cups the hillside monastery
In the curve of its scythe

Like a capital *C* in an illuminated manuscript.
I stand at the edge and let the pea gravel
Slip underfoot and over, all the way down to the city.

A scumble of lead white, coal soot,
And a brush's frayed, fugitive hairs:

New to full, full to new.
The window dark.
The window bellied with light.

At eye-level on the doorjamb,
The brittle jacket of the cicada.

Between a dream
And the residue of a dream,
The body a ghost sloughs.

The hazel rod of the *word,*
The augur of the *landscape,*

Written down in a calligraphy
So elaborate it was illegible:

Serifs, tendrils, knots, serpents,
An umbilical like a noose,
A thicket of thorns and bindweed

Where as a child I cut a tunnel
And in the cool maze of shadows
Slept until nightfall,

The spiders writing another story
In the empty spaces above.

The skiff, unmoored, leaves no mark
As it drifts out with the tide.
The coming storm drags its rain
Like a full net behind it.
If what we share is the waking,
Give me an ampule of dream.

If I squint my eyes I can see the floating world where all
    forms are born.
The white of the birch, the winter's only green, is whiter
    than hoarfrost.
I cast a hexagram of six broken lines. I cheated. Threw
    again.
I threw the I Ching *yesterday. It said there'd be thunder at
    the well.*
The word translated as "coaxed" means literally "as fingers
    change strings."
If I squint my eyes I can see the floating world where all
    forms are born.

Beneath a cirrus of chalk dust,
Beneath a penumbra of erasures:
Word traces, strata of equations,
Scansion marks, the day's lessons.

With a needle, I dig the splinter out:
The sliver, dislodged, minute.
The broken surface, the gist.

The body deciphers grief.
I wake at night to the click of its machinery.

Thus far, I have mapped the frayed fabric of a mirage,
Have let the past sift like bone meal into the soil.
What I had hoped to say was sweet, like lead on the tongue.

STRIKING THE COPPER BOWL TO
IMITATE THE SINGING DRAGON

All evening the dark bleeds through:
A shiver of loosestrife,
Amethyst, then gray,

Rice-paper ink-washed,
An octopus spilled and tumbled
From its nether-lair,

Then overexposed, white,
The drought haze backlit,
Graphic with heat lightning.

Green-scaled, rare, awful,
The song of the dragon
Is an anvil's bell,

A hammer-blow—a cold toll,
Rain-tempered,
A song followed always by rain,

But nothing falls.
Except stars—leached salt,
Bone meal through a sieve,

Cold feral fire.
The wells failed.
The reservoir empty.

EPITAPH

Beyond the traceries of the auroras,
The fires of tattered sea foam,
The ghost-terrain of submerged icebergs;
Beyond a cinder dome's black sands;
Beyond peninsula and archipelago,
Archipelago and far-flung islands,
You have made of exile a homeland,
Voyager, and of that chosen depth, a repose.

The eel shimmers and the dogfish darts,
A dance of crisscrosses and trespasses
Through distillate glints and nacreous silts,
And the sun, like fronds of royal palm
Wind-torn, tossed, lashes upon the wake,
But no lamplight mars or bleaches your realm,
A dark of sediment, spawn, slough, and lees,
Runoff, pitch-black, from the rivers of Psalms.

IMPROVISATION

The only bridge across Wind River is the wind.

This is not a poem, not a suture of words, not a voice without accompaniment.

The poem is what silence instigates: a sanctuary between "The Temptation" and "The Expulsion" furnished with footfalls and echoes, a way station between *rapture* and *rupture.*

Beneath the chandelier, a single wooden chair with a braided velvet cord draped over its arms. The poem is not the chair, but the reconfigured function of the chair: *to be seen.*

The wind rattles around in the heart like a janitor with hours still to go on his shift. And nothing left to clean.

Desire and its generation, its preservation, its fulfillment, its deterioration, its vanquishing, its loss, are the residue of the poem and not its source. When I say *the wind,* I mean *the poem.* When I say *the poem,* I mean *a variable in an equation.* When I say *I,* I mean *a voice without accompaniment.*

No one looking in the goat's eye mistakes it for a human eye. The devil's perhaps. Close enough to be the devil's eye. The little horns and the tuft of beard complete the mask. The poem is the expression of the actor behind the mask. The poem is the human eye that, from the theater's back row, seems goat-like in the devil mask.

Put a line through it. *X* it out. *The wind over the lip of the green bottle. The wind-frayed stamen.*

THE COORDINATES

Ten-thousand worlds in the eye of a deerfly
And I slap it against my thigh nonetheless.
So much for the multiplicities of awe.

For now, the horizon's tin edge separates
The figment of sky from the figment of hills.
The dull mileage between the Rappahannock

And Occoquan is but a blink of an eye.
When did the mere sublime fall out of favor?
When did the ineffable lose the sacred?

A spider bridges the gap between two oaks.
A black snake slips through a cowlick of tall grass.
I map the coordinates, take ragtag notes.

Sometimes I can put two and two together.
The wisteria shrugs beneath wind's weight,
Although I wasn't going to mention the wind,

That ghost-driven given, dry, pollen-thick,
Everywhere at once, then nowhere, where it lives.

THE FLAME

The flame is an object transformed by its displacement.
The flame is a qualm of zags and gnarls.

Between the match and the wick,
The rain turns to hail.

Between the match and the wick,
Pison, Tigris, Gihon, and Euphrates flood their banks.

My father refused to swim.
As a merchant marine, he went overboard

And was forced to cross an icy distance underwater,
A distance measured by a surface of burning oil.

The sky above black with smoke.
He would not even watch us swim.

Elusive, shuddered, shredded by a breath,
The flame unravels a configuration of shadow by which
        the world is known.

If all things are exchanged for fire,
Then there is no bridge over this burning ground.

The souls, as I reach out my hand, lean toward such solidity,
Then gutter like flames, retreat.

In the midst of telling my dream,
I remember only my waking.

The flame is wayward, an afterthought congealed,
Eros courted by Ambivalence, a canker,

The gaze of an icon, a thorn,
A shipwreck in a Romance.

How long has reason darkened my desire?
I hold my hand over the flame.

Between the flame and my hand, an equinox.
Between the flame and my hand, a grain of millet.

Between the flame and my hand,
The shallow night silted in with soot.

THE OLD BRICKYARD ROAD QUARRY

The world begins with a gaze, impromptu,
The first light endlessly divisible,
Starless, submerged in vapor, unscored, loosed,

So that one does not think of proportion,
Abrupt edges, magnetic poles, remnants,
Or, for instance, the quality of mercy,

Or the maker. To dispense with narrative,
To let go of the ledger, the inventory,
The ten-thousand stains where blood redeemed,

Is to believe in the dream's irrational
Counter-history, the limestone scree,
The said and to-be-said held in solution,

The weight a body takes on, inch by inch,
As it's pulled from the quarry's clouded water,
A body bloated, radiant. Jade-tinged. Pearl.

MY MOTHER AMID THE SHADES

If you are my son, what proof do you offer?
I give you the annunciatory angel's lily.
I give you the rubric of Christ's hidden scripture.

If you are my son, these are not yours to offer.
I give you a wine bowl of ivy wood.
I give you four walls of wild pear, a roof of gold.

If you are my son, what proof do you offer?
I give you a field of windfall ripe with wasps.
I give you a single pear wrapped in tissue.

If you are my son, these are not yours to offer.
I give you the story of my father, your husband.
I give you all that was taken from him.

If you are my son, what proof do you offer?
None. The pyre, at last, translated all to ash.
At the border, they took everything, even his name.

CONSTELLATIONS OF AUTUMN

Who oversees this collect of caws, this clamor of crows, gathered by grace around a carcass?

Alas, our narrator is despondent *[from the Latin,* despondere, *meaning 'solemnly to undertake a promise']* and having given his word, has nothing else to give.

It is not the rain that set the star-of-Bethlehem white above the valley. *Hath the rain a father?* It is not rain, but a hillside of white flowers.

Now is the hour for dousing the fire. The curfew. "Too much whiskey these days, late getting up / I lie and watch the western hills, give up on unfinished poems."

Thomas Merton: "A postulant said this morning, 'How deep do they dig a grave? They have been at it all morning.'"

A sudden wind through the summerhouse. The constellations of autumn. The landscape a box of air. An empty reliquary. Error not erased but crossed out.

Aquinas believed poetry the lowliest of the sciences—it has little truth about it. I walk the Post Road and argue with Aquinas. Point out the thistle, the cornflowers.

Who would not curse the snake and its shadow? Who, in finding its papery skin snagged in brambles, does not begin to believe the Resurrection?

When the roll is called up yonder, when the roll is called up yonder, when the roll is called up yonder, when the roll is called up yonder, I'll be there.

Too much whiskey these days. Late in getting up. I lie and watch the western hills. The sun all haze. Read the poems of my teachers and go back to bed.

NIGHT FISHING

My father stepped off the path.
Then my brother. I followed.

Even then I was a collector:
A quail feather, a bolus,
Chips of fool's gold,
Milkweed down, poplar seed.

I knew then as now
The tangible world,
The demands of nostalgia,
The cosmology's concentric circles.

They wait for me
Beside the cow pond
To find my way.

I collected elements for a divination kit:
A thimbleful of rusted filings.
A horseshoe magnet.

I knew then as now
How to read in sand
The movements of a snake.

They are there,
My father and brother.

How to fashion such a night?
Starlight snared in the amnion?

I finger each knot in the net bag
We will use as a creel
And find no flaw, no tear.

I navigate by the twin tips
Of their cigarettes,

The pulse of burn and dull,
Burn and dull:
The distance between us constant.

There must be a word that means
To knock repeatedly
On a door to gain entrance
And yet not gain entrance.

First my father disappears
Into the canebrake.
Then my brother.

READING THE ANCIENTS

I say melancholy is sweet milk when I know it's alum.

The story is always the same: one thing leads to another.

The iris unsheathes behind a screen of rain. A fern stays
furled.

The sparrow hath its home and the swallow its nest. Fair
enough.

How soon the light changes—glare to wan, steeped to
seared to tarnished.

Though no one plays, the piano tuner still comes once a
year.

I like to hear the keys tested, the notes bent back into shape.

It's hard not to envy the practicality of his skill.

For me, for years, depression has been my shelter.

It looks like I'm moving, Bob Dylan sings, *but I'm standing still.*

A DEAD CROW ON GOOD FRIDAY

The wing's torn black iridescence, flint-edged,
Once a dynasty of shimmers and glosses,
Shines, if it shines at all, as rain-slick char in the curfew
      light, the truant light, light that strays.

One could renounce, at this point, the gaze—*look away!*—
But no, the lens has been ground
At great expense and, held at the right distance, magnifies
      and clarifies the tremors and aftershocks,

The tabulation of tenebrous light and shadow,
Shadow and light that stay nothing, that hold
No moment in their moment, the moment verging, mutable,
      unfixed, at once *here* and *hereafter.*

One would expect a gash, as sudden and lush
As the redbud along the spring-fed creek;
One would expect splayed viscera, split ribs, the ribs picked
      clean of maggots by thrush and starlings,

Yet in the crow's cold eye, the malformed sky opens a com-
      pendium of clouds.
In its cold eye, where later ants will forage,
A shadowed valley, one's own inverted reflection, distorted,
      almost familiar.

HISTORY

A hundred flint arrowheads, chipped, rain-washed, scat-
    tered through a meadow of ragweed and clover,
The flesh they ripped, the rib nicked, the shields of horse-
    hide torn, all lost to the elements;
An ice-pierced daybreak through a mica screen and the first
    lute arrives in China from Persia;

The uses of ambergris are perfected; the lamb's blood dries
    above the doorway; a glacier calves an iceberg;
From the rock where a father offered up his son as sacrifice,
    the Prophet ascends into paradise;
The summer you step on a rusted nail, the willows green
    and bend to the river; the river floods;

Before nightfall, a body is bargained for, secreted away in a
    borrowed grave fashioned from a cave;
Again, walls and towers topple. And no language but grief
    is left in common. And grief no language at all.
There is no history, only fits and starts, laughter at the
    table, lovers asleep, slaughter, the forgetfulness.

And yet for three nights straight, nothing but starlight—
    Byzantine, quicksilver, an emanation of a past—
And tonight you have renamed the constellations after
    the mudras: *The Gesture Beyond Mercy,*
The Gesture for Warding Off Evil, The Gesture of Fearlessness,
    The Gift-Bestowing Gesture of Compassion.

MATERIA PRIMA

[small corpus]

There where the thread breaks,
There where the prayers are blown out
With the votives,
                    a zodiac of live coals,
A loose cursive script
Of pine soot ink and clear water
Defining the fog and mountains.

The broken spine of a book
Hinges autumn to winter.

When she touches his eyelids
He shuts them.

The book, a book of songs,
Falls open to:
            the lily among the thorns.
To: *a bundle of myrrh.*

When she touches his eyelids,
When she touches her tongue to his nipple,

He sees a sky as blue as the god's body.

[dance glyph]

The riddle begins: *the deer enters the winter arbor.*
The riddle begins: *the second cutting, the aftermath.*

Her right hand opened in the gesture of forgiveness.
Her left in the gesture of compassion.

The moon—a copper souvenir oxidized to green,
A mottled chip of fallen plaster, mineral-stained—
Is eclipsed by the lamp the sleeping lovers left on.

The riddle begins: *a harvest of frosts.*
The riddle begins: *the orb of air in the spirit level.*

Above them, the analects of stars.

In his dream, the Northern Lights curve away
Like a curl of wood from a lathe.

In her dream, he steps into a skiff
Built to ferry ghosts.

The riddle begins: *the far bank of the river—*

[mask with red]

From the seven windows, she could see the seven moun-
        tains that house the seven gods.
From the seven windows, he watched the smoke, hunkered
        on the river, not rise.

The red: tea of rose petals. Rust. Staghorn of the sumac.
        A pin-prick of blood.
The mask: *kanji* on lambskin. The face of a wind. Consort
        to the barn owl.

From the seven windows, he watched birds steal straw
        from the lawn, leaving seed exposed.
From the seven windows, she could see the seven moun-
        tains that house the seven gods.

When she wore the mask, he could feel her touch every-
        where at once.
When he wore the mask, he stumbled, as in a game of
        blindman's bluff.

[celadon]

How long before the dew basin overflowed,
Before the gauze sleeve embroidered
   With a knot of dragons
Became wind across a stony draw?

He says: *My heart is a cave of spirits.*
He says: *My heart is a splintered sound-box.*
She says: *I know.*
She says: *I know.*

When the crow lifts, a little snow
Shivers down from the branches.

She says: *I love that color.*
Meaning: the dusk air between the apple and pear orchards.
Meaning: the backlit wasp's nest.
Meaning: the glazed shard among the coral and carnelian.

How long before the moon dissolved
Like sugar under the tongue?
      Before the green ice broke up?
Before the creek, swollen with runoff,

Eddied around an oar of orchid wood?

[skull with thought]

At dusk, the channel markers seem unmoored,
Adrift in the drift of the oncoming night.

Always a little song to spin from the pain:
Always a little song to spin from the pain . . .

Her window is unlit. His dream is an abandoned draft,
A watermark below the surface of the seen.

Nothing seems worthy to hang upon the nail,
So it remains the white wall's one ornament.

[materia prima]

She was to him as distance is to a traveler.
He was to her the three compass points not followed.
        That is where the story ends,
And without a mention of *northwest* or *southeast*
Or *how far* or *the one-thousand labors in between.*

The telling begins: *In that time* . . .
And each teller, who might tell the story, goes from there—
        The lead, or bronze, or iron, white hot,
Is poured over the lip of such an overture,
And what we thought was the story,

What took the shape of the story,
Vanishes like lost wax.

[corpus]

Her husband, of course, imagined the god's body
Intertwined with hers,

Merged—a white mineral flame,
Radiant, involuted, churning.

The rest of the story, she insisted,
Was of no account.

He held her through the night,
Through a dream's argument,

Through an August rain
That did not cool the summerhouse.

Her body. My body, he added.
Always two. Joined by *and.* Held apart by *or.*

Later she scattered thistle seed
To attract the mourning doves,

And two came, skittish at first.
She scattered more and they stayed all day.

PIAZZA S. SPIRITO NO. 9

I will always love this light: the brayed clarity of gypsum,
      the cool kiln-glow of amber,
No longer liquid, not yet stone.

And the green shutter creaked by a breeze. And, across
      the courtyard, the laundry pulleyed in,
Echoing a song of rhymes: *toll, coal, squall, straw, strewn* . . .

And the table set with a vase of lavender, the table level on
      the shim of a closed matchbook.
And the sleep easy afterward, the heavy sleep of the body
      unencumbered by dream or memory.

My body cradled in the luminous idleness of your own.

FINAL THOUGHT

What I have argued thus far is but a treatise
On the owl and the moon, as if the given
Were world enough, as if one thousand and one

Views of the moon—each phase marked, inscrutable—
Illumined the hairline crack in the plaster,
The door to the river, midwinter's passage,

A field of view inverted through a pinhole.
The terrestrial and celestial globes
Are not translations of figured worlds,

But worlds figured, where the owl flushed from the oak
Circles above a lost plan of paradise,
The tumbled onyx wall, the enclosure's gate.

All is shaped by the moon's static glare and verge,
Its cold charge, by talon, span, plummet, and swerve.
Awake I read the script of a reverie,

Parse and dissect a reed shaken by the wind,
And asleep the *Ars Magna Lucis et Umbrae,*
The monocle of the shallow fire pond,

The surface lux, lumen, color, and splendor,
Silvers and salts from which the image appears.
Between waking and sleeping, I smudge the chalk

Of the plumb line, behold a heaven so vast
No word can stain it. An object's flawless fact
As it is desired is, in fact, its flaw,

The object's flaw the fact of its attraction:
The mimicry of lack and want, want and lack,
The melancholy of *there is . . .* and *there is . . .*

The owl and moon are points of departure.
Pythagoras read the moon in a mirror,
Divined the future. The owl is my augur:

Talon, span, plummet, and swerve, silence subsumed
Into silence, a final thought that tightens
Like a slipknot around nothing and undoes itself.

Reliquaries (2005)

LIGHT BY WHICH I READ

One does not turn to the rose for shade, nor the charred
      song of the redwing for solace.
This past I patch with words is a flaw in the silvering,
                          memory seen
      through to.
There I find the shallow autumn waters, the three stolen
      pears,
The horizon edged with chalk, loose where the fabric
      frayed.
Each yesterday glacier-scored, each a dark passage illumined
      by a honeycomb.

I begin to fathom the brittle intricacy of the window's
      scrim of ice.
For years, I managed without memory—stalled,
      unnumbered, abridged—
No more alive than a dismembered saint enthroned in two
      hundred reliquaries.
Now, it's hard not so say *I remember,*
                       hard, in fact, not to
      remember.
Now, I hear the filament's quiver, its annoying high
      frequency, light by which I read.

River mist, mudbanks, and rushes mediate the dark matter
Between two tomorrows:
                                   one an archive of chance effects,
The other a necropolis of momentary appearances and
        sensations.
One, a stain of green, where a second wash bleeds into the
        first.
The other time-bound, fecund, slick with early rain.

As if to impose a final hermeneutic, all at once the cicadas
        wind down.
The gooseberry bush looms like a moon: each berry taut,
        sour, aglow.
The creek runs tar in the cloud-light, mercury at dusk.
Then the frogs start up.
                        Clay-cold at the marrow. A
        hollow pulse-tick.
And it seems, at last, I've shed my scorched and papery
        husk.

OWL IN THE VINEYARD

Thought after thought the wheel turns: desire, form,
     formlessness,
And there beyond no-thought, desire.
                                        I listen to the crows
Dicker as they gather in the canopy of a narrow tract of
     woods.
I consult almanacs and star charts.
I put a stick through the spokes, but it does not stop the
     headlong turning.

One must catch the scent of the wolf before it catches one's
     own,
Which is to say, the wind is a variable, and never a constant:
The wind warped by the cedar; wind clenched in embers;
The wind like a midday trance as the horizon is swallowed
     by a snake.
How does the bee ride the poppy in a sun-struck field of
     wind?

I say a prayer for the world and in the midst lose my place
Amid the winter garden, the rain garden,
                            the minor chord
    of seasons.

With grassfire cinders, I smudge in the blur between sky
    and water,
Re-inscribe the coordinates of the unmarked mass graves,
    the road into the forest.
Daily, anonymity and vanity escort me home. Daily, I say
    my prayers.

⁘

Lead gives back little light and what it gives it does so
    sullenly,
Miserly, with an exhausted shrug, neither a bribe nor a
    tribute.
There are times when the fire is mineral and the wind is
    mineral.
There are times when I say *I* when I mean everything I
    am not:
An owl in a vineyard, say, or an unrepentant exile.

THE BACK-STORY

The notebook—benedictions and burlesques, wishes and
    whatnot—is full and closed.
The door, ajar, will slam shut when another door is opened.
                             So much
    for the confessional mode.
I have three parallel scars that run across my lower back
    and no notion of what caused them.
Uncertain of the when and the why, this is the point where,
    by convention, I look out the window
As if the pine, poplar, holly, dogwood and the gravel-filled
    creekbed below were, in fact, a refuge.

The night-fog was like lampblack on curved glass. I drove
    down into the valley and was covered,
Then up again into tree-laden ghost-dark, the pitch and
    grainy green of the forest.
My eyes closed for an instant. Two deer, stark in the head-
    lights, stood, gravity-freighted,
Then flew—apparitions, eidolons, messengers—bright
    antler-tips white gold.
                          My eyes opened
To the shimmy and jar of the shoulder's rumble strip as I
    plunged back down into fog.

I finger each memory as if it were a prayer bead, but each
    crumbles as salt to the touch.
I look at my hands and count a paper-cut, four calluses, a
    blood blister.
                    So much for the epic mode.
All day I make offerings to the shades, wrest whatever clues
    they cleave to.
All day I make offerings to the shades, steal what would
    be given freely were I a shade.
When I come home, my dog lifts her head—not to greet
    me—but to confirm I am the one who left.

"I was driving late, and sure I was drunk," George said,
    drunk and animated, as he recalled the story,
"And there he was, huddled in the middle of the road and
    I couldn't stop and the car thudded
Over him. I killed him, no doubt about it, but the police
    said he had been robbed, and beaten-up
And badly, and left there in the middle of the road for
    dead. I finished him off."
                    George took consolation
In the back-story, in all that was never in his hands to change
    for the better or the worse.

LET ME REST ON THAT PEACEFUL MOUNTAIN

Soon enough I will wash my hands above the spoils, soon
    enough feast among the flies
At a table, daubed and speckled, where my ghost will sit
    before the body it once burdened.
Until then, I transcribe the changes: salt into air, air into
    anthracite, anthracite into fern.
Until then, I watch the creek shrink and fill through the
    seasons.
I watch the moon, cloaked in camouflage, lift like a
    zeppelin.

"Those old songs are my lexicon and prayer book," Dylan
    says of "I Saw the Light,"
"Let Me Rest on that Peaceful Mountain," and "Keep on
    the Sunny Side."
I put on Neil Young's "Only Love Can Break Your
    Heart," TomWaits' "Jesus Gonna Be Here"
And "The Cold, Cold Ground,"
                  and Emmylou Harris's
    cover of Lucinda Williams' "Sweet Old World."
What comfort I feel, though broken and buried, at the pro-
    mise of redemption on this earth which is passing.

More and more I forget the names of things or I'll step into
      a room and forget why I entered.
If I wait, what has slipped catches up with me, the name
      or reason, and I go about my business.
Every day at 5:05 p.m. someone calls, and when I pick up
      the phone, the person says nothing.
Hello, I say once or twice, then we listen to one another
      breathe and neither of us wants to be the first
To hang up, to be the one to let the other have such a
      sublime, mischievous, and useless satisfaction.

A hawk settled and preened on a low-branched oak
      outside the church window.
I was impatient at that very moment with questions of the
      spirit.
Pure in its severity, the hawk turned its head, and though
      I saw its eyes, I did not meet them.
Beyond those wooded acres:
                  the Little River Turnpike,
     the road home.
How often the *out-there* seems a diorama, a lesson in an
      enclosure, an example of the real.

A BIT OF GOLD LEAF

The day of judgment came and went and still the sun rose
    on the dragonflies,
Their traceries' sheen, the needle and silver thread of their
    iridescence.
The day of judgment came and went.
                        I must have missed
    it as I watched the dragonflies' backstitch,
The way they bound the air above the marsh's wind-shifted
    grasses,
Above the sandy bank of Cold Spring Brook as one became
    three, three became seven, seven became thirteen.

I like to imagine the absent objects the hands held, or the
    hands themselves, the mudra of this and that,
The object or gesture that revealed the essential.
                         I overhear
    in a museum cafe from the table next to mine
A mother ask her grown son out of nowhere, "Have you
    ever hated me?"
The spoon lifted from his parsnip soup stalled midway
    between the bowl and his open mouth.
"Oh mother," he complained, "whatever answer I might
    offer to that would have to be a lie."

Everything I put in the attic I should throw away now,
        because what I crick my back and neck for,
Pushing an overfull box of old receipts, ledgers, tax returns,
        bank and credit card statements,
Will have to be hauled down and thrown out.
                                     I stand
        on my tiptoes and pull the thin rope which pulls
The trapdoor down, which unfolds down as a ladder—a
        stairway to heaven it's called.
With the box balanced on my shoulder at the top of the narrow
        stairs, I pull a string but the bulb is burned out.

A bit of gold leaf drifted down as the janitor dusted the
        icon and he watched as the scrap swung on the air,
Hovered, then lifted, spun (the furnace blowers having
        kicked on),
                fell, only to swoop up again,
Glinting, disappearing, white then gold, the size of a torn
        postage stamp.
He stood still and watched it dance over his head, and
        when it reached the door and turned out of sight,
He turned to see me watching, and shrugged, first bewildered,
        then he broke into a smile.

FOUR WALLS AND A ROOF

If I were fluent in another language, I might be fluent at
    last and at least in this one.
When I hear an angel rustle in the matrix of vines and
    hedges amid a thousand thorn spurs,
When the screw-head is stripped and no tool I own can
    turn it,
When I find a pale blue egg fallen, unbroken, in the green
    shade of the shriveled irises,
It is my own wordlessness by which I set down the moment
    and its abracadabra.

Underfoot, the ground gives way to what was a yellow
    jackets' nest, but it is winter,
And what might have been five months ago sorties of
    stings is merely, it turns out, a twisted ankle.
Through a trapdoor, Jesus, having harrowed hell,
                             pulls
    Adam up by the forearm onto stage.
There were times, when I lived on the karst topography
    of Missouri, after heavy spring rains,
The roof of a cave gave way and a sinkhole opened
    swallowing a house, a Black Angus or two.

I put a single poppy seed inside a mason jar, screw on the
    top, and call it *Lethe.*
I put a single pomegranate seed inside a mason jar, screw
    on the top, and call it *Persephone.*
Soon enough four walls are lined with shelved jars—one
    with a spindle in it, one with snake skin . . .
And those who enter the gallery praise the *idea* of the
    project. Not one
Attends to craft, how not a lid is mis-threaded, how the
    shelves are level, the nails countersunk.

Lost in the woods, not acquainted with the sublime, not
    stumbling upon it by journey's end,
I found no clues of East or North in the snow clouds
    ferried on the wind. No sun, no stars,
Not a single landmark visible through the pines,
                                   through
    the twelve acres of oak,
The principalities of the screech owl, no other footprint in
    the vole's leaf litter.
I was lost, not predator, not prey, but I am here and so I
    conclude I found my way.

A TOKEN OR TWO

To hedge his bets, he would build a temple to the unknown
    god— the one unworshipped all those years,
The one whom he had not even imagined, perhaps a
    jealous one, a wrathful one, one left in the cold
Inadvertently.
            If the brevity of a human life is, as the
    Psalmist says, a handbreadth
And if he knew how easily his own hand had turned over
    in anger, frustration, and vengeance,
It was not too soon to break ground, to clear the forest, to
    sink the pilings, to build first the outer wall.

I never would have expected to see the damp, green hay
    begin to smolder, to consume itself,
Flames, at first, green, more smoke than flames, as if an
    ink of soot, oil, and gum of balsam,
To burn as it inscribed the rolled bales into its ledger, not
    as an image, but as an inventory,
Stock against the future, and then the paper itself is char.
                            The herd,
        unperturbed, stood
Bunched together chewing the late spring grass, chewing
    the chewed, until the dog brought them in.

He built the other wall from a ruined Corinthian colonnade
　　　　and filled in the gaps with coral and rubies.
A narthex of sardius, topaz, and carbuncle. A nave of
　　　　emerald, agate, and amethyst. Through the gate
Of a single pearl,
　　　　　　　　an altar of sapphire, diamond, jasper,
　　　　and beryl onyx.
He prepared the altar with offerings of macerated musk,
　　　　civet, and butter, a sheaf of barley,
A token or two he had managed to steal, when all the
　　　　gods were nameless, from a magpie's nest.

I am kin to the crow, cousin to the fire, which tells you
　　　　even less than I previously let on.
I and *he* are not the same, but like the fire and crow are
　　　　bound by a tangle of blood,
Or so I say, preferring to see design in the random,
　　　　preferring to design the random,
As my father must have, retelling a story as if we had
　　　　never heard it.
　　　　　　　　　He forgets himself,
And the one ruined crop becomes the fall of a dynasty, and
　　　　thus he is cast out, a prince without a land.

AS OF YET

After my parents died, we boxed up their clothes, coats,
    and shoes, scrubbed the walls,
Swept up the dust that had grown thick between the gold
    shag carpet and the hallway baseboards.
Shutting the door to their room firmly, I heard the empty
    hangers rattle and jangle in the open closets
Like a gamelan for a shadow-play, a shadow-play in which
    the won kingdom, long after the siege,
Seems hardly worth the hardships, the years of lack, the
    treacheries, the endless soliloquies and asides.

I love best the next-to-last bite, not the flesh above the
    green and the rind, but the stall, the suspension,
The as-of-yet-not-coming-to-an-end, the hunger not
    sated, the musk melon not yet consumed,
The penultimate's flirtation with finale, one foot on the
    brake and one down hard on the gas.
Once, as I looked at an elaborate *trompe l'oeil*—

                                    feast,
    flowers, and fruits of four seasons, dew drops—
A house fly lifted off the crooked claw of a cooked pheasant
    and revealed the fly's painted double beneath.

The names of things—Halftide Rock, Long Sand Shoals,
    Salt Works Bay, Sodom Rock—
Are as true as the degrees between North and True North.
The jellyfish, a thousand lamps, flare and dim, flare adrift:
A depth of dream not seen, but looked into, through, a
    reflection translated as transparence.
A thousand lamps among the zones of darkness. The
    riddle, of course, is do they rise or fall?

The gifts one brings—wildflower bouquets, wines, fruits,
    nuts, wheat—add to the overload.
In the cave of the oracle, a sweet air vents from a fissure in
    the rock—
A surfeit of sulphur and gardenia, the turn of pears from
    ripe to rot—
And held in the lungs, taken in deep and held,
                                            induces
        one to see how the oracle sees:
The tesserae of ivory, glass, and gold as the face of God,
    the mind's random firing as prescience.

BLACKBERRY BLOSSOM

Bob was in love then. We all were. But Bob newly so. And
    because of love, we admitted to happiness.
And in spite of love—the stories we told all night of love—
Our fucked-up parents, old (now) lost loves,

                        the inventory
    of hurts, of crushes.
How blind we had been, how stupid not to leave when the
    door was open.
We talked all night on the sandbar. In our canoes at dawn,
    tired, we let the river do the work.

One need not count the fathoms if one can read the
    diminishing light,
The accumulating cold. Yet seized by reverie, pulled
    down,
One cannot distinguish figure from ground,

                        lightning
    from its afterimage, the daughters of memory
From nine drowned valleys, from gnats that hover head-
    high in multiples of nines,
The nine degrees of shadow for which memory is the
    predicate.

At the end of thought is not memory but the end of thought.
Yet having imagined the end of thought one attempts to
    recollect the negations and embellishments
By which one arrived there.
                                And having arrived, the
    negations and embellishments
By which one might retreat from such terminus, might
    turn and retrace one's steps in back out.
Up ahead the willows bend to the water, as a reader might
    to a page.

As I listen to Norman Blake play "Blackberry Blossom," I
    remember the river
Spread wide over the meadow, the few fenceposts poking
    up weathered silver,
The company of crows that followed us in.
                                Bob was in
    love then.
We all were. But Bob newly so. The serpentine smoke
    from the fire he built lazed and lingered,
As had the thin whorls from his oar as he had navigated
    us out of the narrow rapids to calm.

THE MANDALA AND THE SQUARE

If all phenomena are empty, why does the underdrawing
      bleed through:
A grid of hand-drawn horizontals, lines thinning to where
      the brush is re-dipped,
The verticals snapped lines, the ink thickest at the point
      of impact; the interstices
And hollows patched with indigo's luster, vermillion
      from cinnabar, the red of lac,
Azurite, malachite, and other cuprous minerals on this
      orderly model of the universe?

I cannot dispel the obstacles. Cannot hear the twilight
      language beyond words. Try as I might.
I cannot step outside this well-fed furnace I call a body.
      Cannot account for the hours.
Cannot reconstruct the sequence of events that was the
      day before yesterday.
Cannot confirm my alibi. The long convalescence draws
      to a close. I browse among the ruins.
As I look down, a garter snake slips between the gnarled
      roots of a stump spiked with new growth.

"When I cover the square surface with rectangles, it lightens
      the weight of the square, destroys its power,"
Agnes Martin writes, regarding the hand-drawn grids
      afloat on her six by six canvases.
Yet in the very act of undermining the ideal she reiterates
      the revelations of its perfection.
How does one give in without giving up when one has
      mastered the conventions of closure?
"The way of the artist," she says, "is an entirely different
      way. It is a way of surrender."

I broke a stick of rosemary wood and the resinous
      aroma—a hint of pine bark,
Even lavender, but more mineral than leaf or bloom—
      rose and I breathed it in.
The fragrance did not conjure memory, but had about it
      the essence of the *remembered.*
I sat on the front stoop killing time, almost happy in the
      warmth of mid-March sun,
Desiring this moment and not the next. Welcoming the
      next without desire.

THE NARRATION OF RAIN

Rain blows through the pines. Rain rattles water oak leaves.
    Rain on the stone chime.
Rain quick in rivulets and gullies. Rain on the river's
    broad back. Rain amid rain.
Rain fretting the rusty clay. Rain at a slant. Rain every
    which way but down.
Rain overflows the gutters. Rain marbles the picture
    window. Rain slips, stumbles, sluices.
Rain in the corn crib. Rain in the trough. Rain blows
    through the pine.

      ⌒〜

The crow carries a bauble in its beak—something dully
    reflective—
And drops it onto the path of leaf mulch ahead, caws once,
    and lumbers up and low
Over the gauze of gnats, where wild blackberry overruns
    the unused train tracks.
I will leave the trinket for another to find.
                    I sidestep the
    omen. Ignore the oracle.
Having learned nothing from Sophocles as I put one foot
    in front of the other.

"Assyrians," the husband said, "are the first to use images
    to narrate."
(I eavesdrop in museums, a bad habit, I know, but one I
    prefer not to set aside.)
The wife—I have assumed they are married, long married—
    nods *yes.*
"In archaic art," he says, "human faces are a blank.

                             Emotion
    is given to the hunted animals."
She furrows her brow and nods *yes.* Dubious. Holding
    back some rebuttal.

I have never heard the nightingale nor beheld the manzanita;
I know nothing of the gods: their tedium, their melancholy,
    their blood's leaden sludge.
But I have made a narration of rain as it blows through
    the pines, as it slips, stumbles, and sluices;
The rain as a scattered body; the rain as shape-shifter; the
    rain as blessing;
The rain on the face of the hunter and on the sorrowful
    face of the prey.

EXTRACTS FROM A TREATISE ON FORM

I attempt to make manifest the hidden, and in doing so,
    attempt to not veil the apparent.
Easier said than done. In the painting of the volcano, the
    gray ash plume contends
With the foreground's blossomed spectacle of a bird-of-
    paradise
Rendered in botanical objectivity: orange and blue flowers
    flared on a green spathe.
The volcano, as of yet, not erupted. The volcano, in the
    meantime, a backdrop for the exotic.

Although it is late March, I stand puzzled by an autumnal
    nexus.
I translate desire as its surrogate, the object.
I reduce today and yesterday to salt cantos,
Their order for now orderly, ordinary, as if ordained.
But what is preserved? The austerities, perhaps? The
    rain-weathered remnants?

The stations of the cross, the implements of the passion,
    the wounds;
The five ambrosias, the five illuminations, the eight petals
    of the lotus, the eight perils,

Or, say, the seven hills, the seven rivers, the seven mani-
        festations of fog:
I put down a hash mark for each, not knowing what to
        count and what not to count:
One tooth, two quinces, three amulets, four compass
        points, five retorts.

⁓

I attend to the preliminary maneuvers of wind in the
        juniper,
To how the leaf-dust funnels up off the asphalt and
        resettles,
To how the hawk rides updrafts, banks, patrols the borders
        of woods' edge and creekbank,
As if the part could stand for the whole and the whole for
        the part,
As if the world before my eyes were merely the *seen*
        mediated by the *act of seeing*.

SIENESE VARIATIONS

With candor, the devil (silhouetted, visage effaced, torso
    highlighted with crisscross scratches
As if someone had tried to rid the world of this image of
    evil with an ice pick)
Points down from the height of the temple's crenellation.
    Jesus rebukes the challenge.
Down here, a quorum of pigeons preens and paces between
    a swath of sunlight
And a colonnade of skewed shadows, congregates and
    lifts—one body—subsumed in glare.

The headache keeps me from the apprehension of imma-
    nence.
I stand in the shade of battlements, towers, the wall's
    embrasures, heat-stung, dizzy, disoriented.
Through some gift of intuition, perhaps,
                              I know what it
    is I do not know.
I construct an *I* who senses, in the stark Siena noon, God
    with us,
Among us, in us. By *us* I mean only the *I* and only for that
    instant.

Inch by inch, a story, although unraveled and ragged at its
      end, continues:
The ether of grief transmutes into tears, the tears into relics,
      the relics back to ether.
I spend the afternoon studying Duccio's depiction of the
      entry into Jerusalem.
Is the look of awe on the faces in the crowd the awe of
      wonder or the awe of dread?
I admit I'd be reading ahead if I said this had the look of
      a funeral procession.

I've been known to stand at a height (in a bell tower, on
      the catwalk circumscribing a cathedral's dome)
And to imagine the stepping out and off, the curve of, the
      acceleration of the fall,
And to imagine the distance of the fall

                        as three or four
      seconds of calm anonymity,
Three or four seconds without misgivings, retractions, or
      apologia,
An amplitude of lightness in which, despite evidence to
      the contrary, one seems to levitate.

LINES COMPOSED ABOVE
THE OCCOQUAN RIVER

The past nags like a deerfly that won't be shooed: I
      know its sting, its aftermark.
Melancholy, which once seemed sweet, turns like last
      autumn's cider to vinegar.
My beard has gone gray, but not my heart. Not yet.
Cold wind. A whetted edge of snow in the air.
Nonetheless, the returning birds bring with them sutras
      and psalms.

Silence for all its negations and privations remains adequate
      shelter.
The sun left its mask on the water. The tops of trees blew
      every direction at once.
If I lost a set of keys years ago, then for years I left the door
      unlocked.
The plaster's hairline crack lengthened and zigzagged
      down the wall.
Nonetheless, the returning birds bring with them sutras
      and psalms.

The more I whittle away the *self* the more the heartwood
      shows.
I point to the litter of curled shavings on the ground. I
      conceal the thin stick in my hands.
A thousand and one words to confirm the null, a thousand
      more to illustrate,
A thousand more to compound the conundrums, a thousand
      to surrender.
Nonetheless, the returning birds bring with them sutras
      and psalms.

My beard has gone gray, but not my heart. Not yet.
Although melancholy sharpens and turns, I still recall its
      sweetness.
The wind's fricatives fumble through the undergrowth as
      a stutter that will not give way to a word.
In the hibernal dusk of early spring, I listen as if they will.
I listen to the returning birds. I listen to psalms. To sutras.

OR THORNS COMPOSE SO RICH A CROWN

The greens—kingfisher, fern, cut shoot, mineral—
      constellate amid the understory.
Nicked with new wood, the crab and cherry relinquish
      the cold for the hard knot-work of blossoming.
Wild's ways less a text than ever. A gnarled language
      abandoned long ago. Holy week:
The dead-fall and leaf-fall clutter the path by which one
      might proceed. A far-off dog bark
And the scrupulous whistle of a mourning dove's wings
      foretell the coming travail.

Rain-light, but no rain above the watershed, rain-light
      giving way to night,
Night to a critique of night, propped up on a crutch of
      twin cedars.
For now, numb to contrition, to a fanfare's affirmation, I
      attend to the critique's hypnosis.
Last year's palm fronds are burned to render this year's
      ashes,
Ashes by which the marked are cleansed and the cleansed
      marked.

I stripped back the bark, and the green wood—raw, pierced
      by my thumbnail—smelled of mint,
Of the recollection of mint—faint, crisp, invasive like mint
      itself taking root where it will—
And thus the mint (truly a mere suggestion of a scent)
      seemed more cause than consequence.
Those who expect the miraculous, I've come to learn, find
      it. Those who don't are sometimes surprised.
I sensed other essences—cinder, anise, noon's tin-edge
      heat—but the green wood smelled of mint.

There in the gaps and makeshift rigging of a conjunction—
      the accounting of *and* and *and,*
The narrative of *therefore,* the detour of *however*—is no
      cure, but merely a mind at work,
Saying what it can say within the confines of its strictures,
      on the worn path of its habits.
I cannot corroborate the execution and demise nor the
      reported anomalies at the grave.
Or, I could continue, offer another story made of only the
      versions' contradictions.

THE FOSSIL RECORD

In the fragile late hour of early spring,
                                    I cannot shake the
        cold of imagination.
It is my habit to answer a question with a question,
Not to avoid the answer, but to get closer to an unapproach-
        able answer.
There is no end to errors on this exilic earth,
No end to the fleeting, fragmented memory-ruins upon
        which a vision is engrafted.

The horse twitches one ear. Then the other. The swallows'
        shadows ride the creek line.
The fossil record fails to disclose the prologue, the getting-
        started,
The stratagem that refuses the frugal lexicon of winter.
The horse twitches one ear. Then again the same ear, as if
        to shoo the wind from the muddy lot.
The inexhaustible wind stirring.
                                    Sleeplessly, indifferently,
        democratically, it stirs.

Almost every other year, I have to saw off the padlock and
   buy a new one,
Having forgotten, in the time between, the combination.
But today, the shed door stands open and I have no idea
   what's become of the lock.
What's inside? A couple of broken mowers, three rat
   traps along the wall, a legion of crickets
And some junk the previous owner stored believing
   someday it would come in handy.

Memory is a bolus of sharp-edged bones, matted fur,
   gristle, and buckshot.
I study the indigestible as if from it I might read the days
   to come, the kingdom come.
I study the indigestible as if from it I might piece together
   an effigy and burn the past.
The little spur of the moon scratches the window that
   looks out over the marsh.
By moonlight, I meditate upon the intricate differences
   among et cetera and et cetera and et cetera.

DEEP RIVER (2008)

AS A DAMPER QUELLS A STRUCK STRING

To name the melon flower is not to chart the hypothetical,
Nor tame the fledged edges of the wild.

To name the melon flower
(Two words calling forth a globe and dried-out vines)

Is to feel in one's mouth dusky vowels.
The words, beyond the drone of logic,

Are barely there.
A hint as of a fragrance,

A concoction of sulfur, brine, charred driftwood, and rose:
Less than a dash, more than a pinch.

Is it for nothing, then, that the wind's
Tributaries stall, baffle and fall, at the horse latitudes,

While the wind here troubles the hill's tiger lilies,
Glazes then roughs up the pond's surface,

Fabricates from roadside sand
(Gone before I can name it) a cyclone?

THE THOUSAND THISTLE SEEDS

Ten years ago, I followed a lizard
Through a grassy, ruined amphitheater,
Quick as quicksilver,
But green, not silver.
The lizard darted,

Skimmed, froze,
Shinnied, insinuated like flame,
A pinpoint of pulse and flash.
The lizard knew
The Etruscan wall's cracks,

The downspouts,
The stone that blunts the plow,
The mortar's and stucco's flaws.
The lizard dwelt in a present
That extends, elongates, thins

Into a filament of consumed air.
I followed the lizard
From brick chink to olive grove,
Poppies to straw,
To sand and loam.

I knew, for a moment, the balance
Between the intimate and the infinite,
        A word and what it reckons.
The sun on the hilltop
        Flared upon the thousand thistle seeds,

The thousand virtues,
        The thousand minerals,
The thousandth of a second
        It takes the lizard to taste the moment
And change course.

TWELVE VIEWS OF A LANDSCAPE

1.
The itinerant season shuffles through the litter of days.

2.
Call it *the hour of the starlings*. Call it *the empty chair's enigma*.

3.
The clouds move like dreams moved before fire's invention.

4.
Avoiding the landscape is no antidote to Romanticism.

5.
Glyphic motifs: winter-revealed clarity, a leafless snare of
    vines.

6.
There in the ensuing emptiness the distance fades as distance.

7.
There is no middle ground: the moon waxes and wanes,
    yet is the same moon.

8.
The landscape like time occurs in an apparently irreversible
    succession.

9.
Call it *the weightlessness of direction.* Call it *the weightlessness
    of direction.*

10.
Memory congeals, hardens as amber around the archaic self.

11.
The body recalls itself as *body* as it moves through the
    landscape.

12.
At noon, shadow, like a tourniquet, tightens at the base of
    things.

SPLENDID THINGS

The word for *rain,* the words for *autumn skies,*
Still legible on burnt paper.
Twice the owl's one note. The dead of winter.

Figments and fragments. An arrow's release.
A dropped quiver, a spill of arrows.
The sledge's bell tone, the thud of the wedge.

A lanky hollyhock. A vine's willful work.
Sketches and notes: a mist-blurred pine stand,
Four seasons on a four-fold screen,

Glacial scratches and gouges on granite.
The half-rhyme of *doubt* and *debt.*
Prairie fires and high clouds.

Starlings and grackles. Grackles and crows.
The horizon's tightrope cut down at night.

UNFORTUNATE THINGS

Gnawed by mice, an organ's leather bellows.
An offer reconsidered, rescinded.
Three wishes, four wives, a world of debt.

Burnt acres, shallow latrines.
To be of two minds, to have half a thought.
The grave for Jesus not even a rest.

A secret that surfaces unbidden.
The unanticipated side effects.
The *in lieu of,* the struck quarter hour.

The infestation, the fumigation.
Trick mirrors, *déjà vu,* a well gone dry.
The bones of a battlefield tilled under.

A used noose. Judas dragged down by dogs.
The mythic reduced to a summary.

THE CULTIVATION OF THE WHITE ROSE

The rose itself,
A slur of moonlight in a horse's eye,

Is chalky, skeletal,
As if distilled from glacial till and birch.

Grown in ash,
It glints with a nimbus of mica.

Grown in clay,
It smells of cold harbors.

Grown in sand,
It opens to reveal a river,

Water that falls,
Descends, levels, and falls.

Its white is edged
With cobalt and erased notations.

Absorbed in sleep,
One dreams of its imperfect white—

Hermetic, fossilized,
Wintered, a concoction of spider silk,

As numb as a phantom limb.

MARSH FIRE

The mind of pure mind is as mutable as azoth. Amid
    lightning
Shadows amber. In the posthumous world. In the now.

Ten thousand threads of thought, Po-Chu-I writes. Mine have
    bitten, ragged ends.
I say one thing and mean another. I say two things and mean
    the one.

The marsh fire—monolithic, archaic—salts the air with embers.
The *I*—neither mind nor body—concocts itself from mind
    and body.

The fuse of the marsh fire down to the creek. The fuse of
    fire down.
Rain and wind collapse like a scaffold of rain and wind.

A cross word. A cross word in a crosswind beyond the
    arcana of glooms and glows.
Beyond the tamp of evening's cold sledge. Beyond the
    claims of crows.

The self is always the problem, tipping the scale this way
    and that.

A murk of lampblack and pitch. A crosswind crossing out
        the changes.

Sunday mirrored in a mirror of Sundays, wed to memory.
        Wed to regret.
Out of focus, a verge of verdigris, a glint-scoured estuary.

Remember how the storm gave way to a bristle of thorns?
New growth darns the charred marsh. A fuse of green down
        to the creek.

226

BETWEEN WARS

A silver crown of flies turns above the mare's head.

Her ears twitch, each on its own, at the least touch of wind.

Fire burns us all, but some more slowly than others. Than
    the next.

The sky, reflected in a tire track's blank and stagnant water,
    is poker-faced.

If a thing can be thought it can be invented. Go ahead and
    say it:

The bodies in the mass grave look like bodies in a mass grave.

You are embarrassed for them: the entwined limbs, this
    one facedown

In the crotch of that one, that one's skirt hiked up to her
    armpits,

The haphazard, unseemly tumble of it all.

Like you, I am dismayed how the unthinkable is always
    thinkable.

Like you, I am in the midst of a long convalescence. You
    would like to re-dress them:

Comb the girl's hair. Cover the boy's gouged skull with a
cap.

The mud and blood are interchangeable. Horseshit dries
in the sun:

Grainy, sage-tinged oats, savory like a shovelful of turned
earth.

THE BODY AND THE LANDSCAPE

I am fluent in a language of stammers.
The world I call *the world* is furtive: ruin and remnant.

Black in drizzle, the woods appear deeper, forbidding.
How diminished, like a fallen hawk, the sublime is.

If, I say, certain of the leverage and counterbalance of the
    then.
How sweet, how bitter the lifting and the descent.

I copy from a primer the day's vocabulary
And call forth the dark and darkening woods in just such
    words.

PASTORAL

The shepherd followed the wolf here along deer paths.
In doing so, he found the city of his birth in ruin.
He had lost track of time.
                              When did the three fire-ponds
        silt in?
When had the ax made its way through the nine orchards?
How long had autumn lingered on the threshing floor?
If he knew the wolf's language, he would ask the wolf.

PASTORAL INTERIOR

I keep to myself. I keep quiet.
I keep quiet. I keep to myself.

The water in the glass is darker than the glass.
The water is heirloom silver left to tarnish.

I keep calibrating the gravity of minutia.
I keep a secret as if it were an antidote.
I keep time by the slow work of rust,

By words cut loose from their moorings:
Cove, clove, cleave . . .

I am listening to "May Sheep Safely Graze,"
As the water in the glass grows darker than the glass.

The twilight—vestigial, lupine—lingers.

FIELD NOTE

An arctic, oblique light—
Grave, earthward—
Roughs in a snowfield's scoured basin,

A curved pine-flecked horizon,
As if onto a province
The door of an Advent calendar

Opened—parenthetical,
Whispered as an aside,
Tallies and marginalia

Erased, yet readable still
In the sleet-lacquered gullies
And scored rock,

A province severed
From the present,
Marooned in the tectonic

Slippage, in the stress
Fractures of the mythic.

THE ANATOMY OF MELANCHOLY

It is not the object, but the loss of it I recall.

Neither the hull of a Hellenistic barge
(Worked from timber felled in autumn)

Nor the angles by which a circle is drawn

Will coalesce as a single thought
Or even reveal a trace
Of the process by which I arrive at

A paper fan half-open, held loosely.

The fatigue of being oneself—
Groundless, without imperative,
All symptom and duration—

Dissipates as manageable boredom.

"How far back the ancient past seems now,"
Montale writes.

By way of anomaly
I begin to see the trace of a pattern.

How far back.

THE BOOK OF CHANGES

The lake ice groaned beneath the car's weight,
But held.
              The long exposure of night hours
Made legible the viscous dark,
The shoal of stars, the frost-flecked docks,
The radio tower.
                   I surveyed the acreage of moonlight,
Took preliminary notes toward an opus posthumous.

The sky—cold-infused—coppers,
Drabs to zinc and tin.
                 My shadow, trapped in ice
An ice age ago, will not budge.

Are the materials at hand negligible?

No farmhouse for miles. Just sky. Stingy light.
Winter's cramped quarters. Stubble-stitched fields.
Calendar squares Xed out as nights pass.

          Which weighs more:
A barn owl's feather or this snow-light?
Wind down the mountain
Or the grit and slag of my small heart?

The world is a world of relics,
A world fused to otherworldliness,
Hammered flat and airy like silver leaf.

The brief moment to which I am native
Fatigues and tears.

Page after page dated,
But nothing like a story emerges.

The crescent moon like a heel scuff,
But no *whereas,* no *because.*

The book is always finished.
The book is always finished

Or almost.
Night stretches above the peaks

Like strings above frets.
Nothing like a story emerges.

The book is always almost finished.

After the flood, five caskets
Float past Ste. Genevieve.
                              And then it is winter:
A sleet-soaked fox lopes across the path,
Head down, tail down, into the thicket.

In the distilled distance,
                              which is home,
Dark windows hold and reflect what they lack.

I read the landscape as a book of changes
And find changes,
                              provisional and preparatory,
A *tomorrow* knit to the abbreviated *now*.

A few stitches dropped.

The air is heavy, as if one too many
Stars occupies the sky.

All winter I did not see a single deer.
In late February, I walked the woods' edge
And found the twenty-pound lick whittled down,
More gray than the last scraps of snow, a mere fist of salt.

In the moth-thin shade
Scutched from green, from flint,
From scurf, from dust—

The clench of a blind grub—
Curl of nacre and slime—
Swollen, bloated, split along the seam

Amid dry pine needles.
On the curved verge of death or change,
(I cannot say for sure)

The grub—not a whit or iota—
Incandesced. Caught my eye.
Once, I compared my heart to a grub,

Or rather said *a cold grub*
Burrowed in at my heart.
Perhaps I was right. Perhaps wrong.

All I know is it is gone
And I cannot begrudge the change
Or changes, the mordancy that remains.

Clouds above the watershed.

Cloud reflections lodge thought-like
In the empty mind of the lake.

Sound carries over water.
                              Tonight, a waltz.
Yesterday, weeping. Tomorrow?

A moment is distinct as it disintegrates,
Enclosing, as it does, the proportion of its vacancy.

A trickle of ground water quarries a cave.
Where a garage stood, a sinkhole opens.

All summer passes like the flash of a bluegill
Pulled from the Blue River.
                              Or was it the Little Blue?

Odd, isn't it, that light is created days before
An eye that might behold it, and an eye taking it in

Changes it to a stray ivory flame,
A labyrinth of two mirrors.

Today, one-quarter of the sky is bright in sun,
Yet rain falls, gives shape to the in-between.

Over time, ornament transmutes
From lotus to palm to acanthus tendrils.
Form is the history of form:

Repository and map— a past intact.
"There is no way to make a drawing,"
Richard Serra says, "—there is only drawing."

Viscera, a gesture, a gesture's restraint:
The body, a mark in time, marks time.

Some hours are not worth counting.

Some fade like a crown of oleander.
Some linger: dragonflies above a drought-shrunken creek.

Some are the long pause of August.

Some you can read as marginalia.
Some as tentative premonitions.

How long can I wait to see
A sheaf of grain as a recurved bow,

Ether's weight gathered
As the droop of willow catkins,

The pearl and flame as the transcendent and tangible?
Soon enough the word

Incarnates as a burnished body;
Soon enough the narrative splits

Into multiple tales of simultaneity,
Into slippages and mudslides,

The grasped and the glanced,
Luck and its finite operations

Chanced upon.
I rest for now after the *et cetera,*

More patient than not,
Out of breath as if I were pulling

Hand over hand from the water's depth
What may just be a bag of bricks.

The stop-gap stitches where the narrative frays
Hold on, even now.

I could plot the days on a grid, assign value
To the x and the y.

As a river of haze lazes above the Blue Ridge,
Edges outline in shadow.

A hawk-call seems a thing made of water:
Salts in solution, lachrymal.

Latent in the *to be,* the past marks a page
And closes the book.

If, as Wallace Stevens argues, the negations are never final,
Then the latticework of birdsong and the evergreen hour,
Like the possibilities beyond the ellipses, can be subtracted
From the whole,
                    yet remain irreducible.

Cranked up from a well's dark, a bucket
Fills with light and, overfull, does not overflow.

AUGUST NOTES

Haze down in the valley. Like flames drawn long,

                                                                pines
    line the hilly horizon.
Born of dust, at home in dust: the pale fossil of the sun.

                                                                              ⌒

All I remember of our last drive together:

                                                                roadside sumac
    slack in heat;
George pulls onto the shoulder near Arrowrock, takes a piss.

                         ⌒

I was young and thought the words would surface
Like a body in a lake.

                    Otherworldly. Not right for this
    world.

                         ⌒

In the out-takes: all I thought I had said,

                                                                all I thought was
    scripted.
All day the dog barks at something I can't see.

At the intersection of the vertical and horizontal fold in
        the map
Is where I'm headed.
                    There where a hole has worn through.

The book will never end,
                        what with the footnotes and
        indices.
The way an oar appears from water, stars rise.

After George shot himself in his truck, a friend—his, not
        mine, not mutual—called.
I said, "Who knows what he was thinking."
                            His friend
        replied, "Who docsn't."

The book of mica crumbles; thus is lost the common mysteries
Of pyrites and limestone,
                              the common idiom of wind in
          Washington, Missouri.

                    ∼

On the scuffed floor of the Legion Hall, a circle of folding
          chairs,
A circle of folding chairs
                    yet to be put away.

                    ∼

August notes: a cicada's wing pinned by a thorn,
                                        crows
          rehearsing
Their doctrines of ash, their theories of soul-making.

                    ∼

George picked up the long-neck empties that rolled around
          on the floor mats,
Hosed out the bed,
                    waxed the truck that day, went for a
          drive.

                    ∼

Not a nocturne, but a night roughed-in with burnt cork:
Whether a short life or long one,

                                    the distances

        foreshorten, cramp.

Stoned, George and I sing along with Neil Young on the
        car radio:
An ambulance can only go so fast.

                                It's easy to get buried in the
        past.

SELF-PORTRAITS

[Without a Subject]

He carries winter within him: a book's clasp shut and
     locked.

He, he calls himself to postpone his own belatedness.

He forgets the map; when he looks down, there it is:
     drawn on his palm.

Once, he fell asleep to a nurse's footfalls in an unlit ward.

Once, he fell asleep to the drizzle-ridden solace of a solstice.

On the rungs: frost.

On the tent above the dug grave: frost.

Frost on the needle and pinched thread.

He carries winter within him: foreclosed, stricken.

He, he calls himself to draw attention away from the worn
     path to the antecedent.

[With God]

He lives inside himself: a bit cramped, but he fits.

His shadow, a byproduct of being, puddles underfoot.

Before he learned to swim, he mastered the dead man's
float.

He finds hindsight is the best sight.

Mesmerized by the allure of surfaces, he admits only to the
null and void.

He can hold his pose in freeze tag long after the game has
ended.

Unflapped in the face of stimuli, he brings the same dish
to every potluck.

Once God filled him: molten steel poured into a casting mold.

At the public swimming pool, he sank like a hunk of metal.

On the bottom, as his breath gave out, he called out to the
coincidence of blues.

[With Good Reason]

As preamble *and* benediction, he cleared his throat.

Not knowing what to say, he said nothing.

The sky, without the moon, seemed to have lost a button.

He said nothing.

For a while, he was depressed and did not know it.

For a while, he was depressed and knew it.

He mustered a little interest in what Mallarmé called *fury
   against the formless.*

Rust kept him company, rust and the faucet drip, rust and
   the river's arterial light.

He stood at the aisle's end as the processional began.

With good reason to hope, he thought the play just might
   be a comedy.

[With Drawn Shades]

Vision begins before and beyond the limits of intellect.

He longs for a shadow to pass across a neighbor's drawn
shade.

Sometimes you find him crouched there in the blind spot.

Sometimes you find him there, an apparition in his own
story.

Sometimes you find him there, snared by the thrall of the
beheld.

The eyes and hooks hold the gaze to the gaze-worried
object.

The eyes and hooks affix the subject to its shopworn erotics.

He is like Jimmy Stewart in *Rear Window,* caught looking.

He is like Jimmy Stewart in *Rear Window.*

Caught looking, he looks away.

[With a Fixed Point]

He lets go of his stinginess.

The provisional, as it is received, is relinquished.

A vast distance opens around the fixed point of the self.

Tonight, a page shivers but not without wind.

Tonight, a snake coils three times around the moon and
gives in to a cold-blooded sleep.

A tally of answered prayers, he knows, can only disappoint.

His childhood dream was invisibility and many times since
then he has gone undetected.

In this ephemeral Elysium, there is only the mere and the
meantime.

The tightrope sags beneath his weight, almost touches the
floor.

For now, arms extended from his sides, palms up, he is a
balanced scale.

[With a Single Footnote]

Like others, he was born to cast a shadow.

He goes, if he goes at all, incognito and wears a blur of
    whiskey.

He is fluent in the forty-four euphemisms for death, thirty
    of which are comic.

A preface to exile is all he managed as a scholar.

The single footnote references something he said once that
    made the whole room laugh.

He knows his words are like the faintest graphite beneath
    a pale blue wash.

He rids himself of apparatus and accoutrements.

To be a shape made of radiance, he would reconsider his
    career goals.

If he ever flared like the oily flame from a fire-eater's mouth,
    no one stopped in amazement to question the
    how or why.

With the intimacy of a shared match (if he burns at all),
    he burns.

[With an Intercepted Letter]

He tried to recollect the past.

He exhumed: *milk gone bad, a nail pulled from his foot.*

Tired, he slept until the sun angled in like a tent spike.

Tired, he slept until he heard a single grackle amid the
    prophetic chattering of grackles.

He weighed less than an idea, than the shadow of gnats
    that kept him company.

Given a choice, he preferred the vowel over the consonant,
    the posthumous over the prescient.

Like a letter stumbled upon (never meant for his eyes) that set
    the crisis in motion, a new day slipped under his door.

Tired, he posed for his funeral portrait.

If he drew, he drew from memory.

If he drew, he drew to remember.

[With River]

His story spreads out like an alluvial fan, plotless.

He tethers a rope of water to a rope of water.

In retelling the story he discovers it to be a Byzantium of
    artifices.

He courts the annulments of cause, the algorithms of
    chance.

What he cannot foresee, he tells in real time.

The river water is cool where it runs, tepid where it stills
    and stalls.

He scans the file for error and finds a brackish wind.

Out of scrap paper, he builds a basilica for the hornets.

Out of colluvium, he builds a cairn at the river's high mark.

He scans the file for error and finds error.

[With the Delectable]

Sometimes he stops just to acknowledge the pain in his
    chest where his heart is.

Sometimes he stops to listen to his vestigial ticker *tock*
    tocking.

He backfills the past with forgetfulness.

Whatever the tedious task or bereavement, his dream heals
    over the moment he wakes.

The moment he wakes, he frets.

He roots around like an old hog knowing something will
    turn up, although most likely not delectable.

What he wants to know is never indexed, never cited.

He takes figments as figures, adds them to the *Assets* column.

He opens the door to discover a spectral world, but finds
    instead misshapen hangers on the rod.

He envies the old poets their *O's, Lo's, Hark's,* and *Ah's.*

THE MISDIRECTION OF A TITLE

I admit I admire the inutility of beauty,
The baroque (from the Portuguese, *barroco:*
         Rough shaped pearl) ambiguities,

Ornate overlays and ambivalences:
A spare coral spiral coffined in glass,
         Erotic Victoriana,

Empirical phenomena,
A green paste of arsenic,
         Spruces in the aspect of winter,

The misdirection of a title.
No evidence is immaterial,
         Not the palm-sized psalter,

Not the burnt-out road flares.
Consider the blue blotting paper
         Bleached like the side yard's hydrangeas,

The Venetian rope-work
Of fogs and drizzles,
         Or these four walls of sheer Virginia rain.

Paradox is not a stalemate
But the integral integer:
         Enigma latent in the commonplace.

Arcane, unused, a plank of vinewood
Warps in the dank garage.
          The gilded, plaster gargoyles

Of the long-ago gutted movie palace
Still loom as the lights dim.
          Beautiful, isn't it,

The distance and proximity
Inherent in a sacrifice,
          In the least of gestures.

SENTENCES (or THE STUDY OF BEAUTY)

Once, I courted the vagaries of intuition, but now, like a grub widening a path through a leaf, I want something to show for my effort, even if only damage.

I swallow the mockingbird whole, yet cannot sing.

If, as Baudelaire says, "[T]he study of beauty is a duel," remember there is not a challenger at the trigger-end of the other pistol, no second to haul the corpse away.

In the Grand Canal's dredged sludge: a ruby and sapphire, china shards, oxidized coins, trace amounts of mercury once used to treat the syphilitic.

I am one of the gods, but have yet to throw off my camouflage of stink and flesh.

At the locus of scrutiny, I change course.

What I move through surrounds me as I press toward a sentence's closure, moving as one might through the world, knowing the mountain laurel first as an aroma, the sycamore as shards loosed by touch, the raccoon as the mulberry stain of its scat on a limestone bluff.

Built on what remains of the ephemeral, the beautiful is obstinate, adamant matter.

THE EFFIGY I CALL MY BODY

My heart hangs, amuletic, where it should
And though I imagine it calcified, inert,

It labors, as is its habit, doggedly.
Attached to the world, I prefer no afterlife.

I slough this body, daily, cell by cell,
Its abjection barely noticeable.

SPIRITUAL EXERCISE

The day set down hour by hour
Like a mortarless stone wall
Ends here: a nocturne of half-tones.

Some nights the interior lights
Butcher the shadows.
Some nights the light itself is flayed.

If each word bears a blessing,
Then I am blessed
On this hand-wrought world,

This austere stage without spectacle
Where the spirit exists in the ritual object
Only for the span of the ritual.

The pines pitch toward evening,
Swaybacked. The compost pile is cold:
Sogged, unturned, a sloth of rot.

Doubt shadows belief, even doubt
Of doubt by which I situate myself.
A fog of broken forms haunts

The woods' edge, or so it seems
Through the smudge of memory
I recast in the present tense.

I can survive in a dwindled space,
Wait patiently for the rendezvous
At *nothing-left-to-subtract.*

Later, one reading these words
Might recognize them for what
They were: fugitive remnants.

One might imagine, as I
Imagined, the project's grandeur.
What I envisioned seems now

Evasion: vagrant moods—
Distilled, abstract, spare—
In a demythologized world.

Today, the mockingbird cribs
Freely from the blue jay and wren.
Their calls absent, yet lucid.

CORPUS HERMETICUM

Beyond scrub and mulberry:
                         an altar of pines,
A year, but only a day or two recalled,

And then only piecemeal:
                         a fallow field
Winter-dulled, a lean horse

Subsumed in fog,
                   yet if I lay a grid
Over the ineffable, place a pin on,

Or scatter a covey of marks across
The surface,
                   nothing is held down,

Or, at least, not for long:
                         the swing's chains rusted,
The slack seat black with mold,

The full moon like a ghost-poppy;
                         and if,
Through the lens of a needle's eye,

I watch a new storm form on Jupiter,
I do not translate the moment,
                         but overwrite it:

Make of words
                        a contingent cosmology,
An archipelago of cast seeds.

SMOKEWOOD CREEK

Crows in the catalpa.
The dog dawdles, laps up fallen mulberries.

Pulls back on the leash to feast on some more.
Each morning the path, restrung with webs,

Offers a new way through the understory.
The creek, swollen with five days' rain, continues

Without thought of origin or end.
A long time's passed since I held a single thought

In my head that wasn't a question.
I follow the dog that follows the path that follows the creek.

RESTLESS GHOST

The wasps' paper nest hung all winter.
Sun, angled in low and oblique,
Backlit—with cold fever—the dull lantern.

Emptied, the dangled nest drew him:
Gray. Translucent. At times an heirloom
Of glare, paper white as burning ash.

Neither destination nor charm, the nest
Possessed a gravity, lured him, nonetheless,
And he returned to behold the useless globe

Eclipse, wane and wax. He returned,
A restless ghost in a house the wind owns,
And the wind went right through him.

BLACKBIRDS, CROWS, GRACKLES, AND RAVENS

The bars of the blackbird's wings flash like Pentecostal
   tongues.

An unlatched door bangs in the wind.

The wind rummages through a hundred acres of sunflowers.

Clothespins ride the perch of a laundry line up and down.

Crows —efficient, inscrutable—make fast work of a road-kill.

Through the rain, the saved and to-be-saved haul folding
   chairs to the Revival tent.

The creek runs with runoff; the creek sags with sediment.

Black leaves in a charred tree, grackles bicker—their racket
   like the rattle of coal in a bucket.

Beyond the Tilt-A-Whirl, as motion predicates, carnival
   lights drag and pearl, derange a little.

If you send forth a raven, you get back what ravens gather.

DEEP RIVER

The river rubs against timbered bends,
Against sheaves of shelved limestone,
Sloughs, silvered with use, its skin,
Its cold spirit of ether and venom,

And approximates a revision.
The river unbodies its body's limits.
Soon enough, trope and figure,
Through common entropy, break down.

Soon enough one blinks
Or turns away. Soon enough
One's hypnosis is cut short
And *river* is river, remains river

Until the deadweight of revery
Pulls one again down:
The river, all mouth and hunger,
Swallows oxbow, flood plain,

Watershed, and promontory
From which one stood and gazed
A gaze transformative, fictive:
Conundrum and confirmation.

The river— hardened, quartz-flecked,
A dark scoured slab— is a river of forgetfulness.

Sun down. Mars on the rise, closer,
Brighter than it's been for ten-thousand years.

The seasons close in upon themselves:
A folio of years foxed and yellowed.

I took what would suffice. I took
What would suffice until nothing would suffice.

One can name a river without mapping it. One can map a
river without naming it.

Remember the water, silt-freighted, slows, delays.

Remember the river owl affirms nightfall with its *too true,
too true.*

If, as Dante argues, love moves the sun and other stars, what
then moves a river?

To name a river is to enter it into history. To step into a
river is to enter its history.

If one stands above where the river converges with another river, or if one stands on the mud flats and in the rills where the wide river transubstantiates into the wide water of ocean— its ghost of green disappearing into a body of salt and blue— the river's name remains the same.

If one could measure a river one would measure the arrivals and departures of the *now*.

Remember that whatever you name a river *(The Silver-In-Which-We-See-Ourselves-Behind-The-Glass, The Night Chase, The Little Rapids . . .)* the name is not a bridge to cross, not a skiff in which to follow the current.

Name the river daily. Forget the river's many names.

The river harbors thunder. The thunder is brusque with flood half the year, shrunken with drought the other half.

At the end of the world, the river splits: one branch into evening, one branch into fire.

Nameless, one can enter the underworld by way of a river.

The river is a reason without language and as such tempts one to name it.

Sub-zero. The sky tin where it rests on the ridge.
The mountains more gray than green, salted with old snow,
Gray as the pigeons that dart from chimney to steeple,

Steeple to steeple to chimney and rest.
The cold holds down the diesel fumes. The cold holds
    itself down.
Downshift and rumble: the trucks slow through town but
    do not stop.

Memory. Memory is all I brought with me here
And the same old desire to name the affect and the
    particulars,
How ice turned to snow and back to ice as I sat at the
    window

Overlooking the river's frozen surface.
A skunk slipped beneath a porch's broken lattice.
A couple of kids spit from the bridge,

Then pointed to something I could not see or guess at.
You might say I was happy in that moment.
I didn't know it just then. That I was happy.

ACKNOWLEDGMENTS

I offer my deep gratitude to The Academy of American Poets and Mark Strand for selecting my first book for The Walt Whitman Award, and my deepest gratitude to the book editors who have supported my work with their labor and faith: Harry Ford for *For the New Year, Heartwood, Apocrypha,* and *The Late Romances;* Harry Ford and Ann Close for *Cenotaph;* Roger Lathbury for reprinting *Heartwood;* and Chase Twichell for *Oracle Figures, Reliquaries,* and this current book. I offer belated thanks to several of my teachers who gave me generous and kind attention over the years: Barry Kincaid, Frank Higgins, Stan Harris, John Robert Barth, Thomas McAfee, Larry Levis, Marcia Southwick, Donald Justice, Henri Coulette, Marvin Bell, Gerald Stern, and Stanley Plumly. I would like to thank the Ingram Merrill Foundation, The National Endowment for the Arts, and the John Simon Guggenheim Memorial Foundation for fellowships, Washington University for a travel grant, and George Mason University for a faculty study leave and for the Heritage Chair in Writing, all of which provided me support, time, and space to write the poems included here. My thanks to Jennifer Atkinson, José del Valle, John Drury, Jeff Hamilton, Jane Hirshfield, Jason Sommer, Allison Funk, Steve Schreiner, Chris Tanseer and Chase Twichell for comments along the way on the new poems in *Deep River.*

Some of the new poems appeared originally in *The American Literary Review, The Antioch Review, Bat City Review, Cervena Barva Press Postcard Series, Field, The Green Mountains Review, The Hayden's Ferry Review, Image, The Iowa Review, The Kenyon Review, Meridian, The Nebraska Review, The New England Review, Sou'wester, Subtropics, Temenos, 32 Poems, Witness,* and *The Yale Review.* A number of the new poems also appeared in a chapbook, *Objects and Mementos* (2007), from The Center for the Book Arts in New York City.

Ausable Press is grateful to

The New York State Council on the Arts

The National Endowment for the Arts

The New York Community Trust

for their generous support.